Proactive
Pastoral Care

Other titles from Bloomsbury Education

Leading on Pastoral Care by Daniel Sobel

Lighting the Way: The case for ethical leadership in schools by Angela Browne

Live Well, Learn Well: A practical approach to supporting student wellbeing by Abigail Mann

Succeeding as a Head of Year by Jon Tait

The Wellbeing Toolkit: Sustaining, supporting and enabling school staff by Andrew Cowley

Proactive Pastoral Care

Nurturing happy, healthy and successful learners

Maria O'Neill

BLOOMSBURY EDUCATION
LONDON OXFORD NEW YORK NEW DELHI SYDNEY

BLOOMSBURY EDUCATION
Bloomsbury Publishing Plc
50 Bedford Square, London, WC1B 3DP, UK
29 Earlsfort Terrace, Dublin 2, Ireland

BLOOMSBURY, BLOOMSBURY EDUCATION and the Diana logo are
trademarks of Bloomsbury Publishing Plc

First published in Great Britain, 2021

A catalogue record for this book is available from the British Library

ISBN: PB: 978-1-4729-8043-4; ePDF: 978-1-4729-8042-7;
ePub: 978-1-4729-8045-8

2 4 6 8 10 9 7 5 3 (paperback)

Typeset by Newgen KnowledgeWorks Pvt. Ltd., Chennai, India
Printed and bound in the UK by CPI Group (UK) Ltd, Croydon CR0 4YY

To find out more about our authors and books visit www.bloomsbury.com
and sign up for our newsletters

Dedicated to pastoral leaders, the unsung heroes of education systems, who empower young people to take charge of their lives, and to my parents, who empowered me to go after my dreams.

Thank you.

Who have you empowered today?

Contents

Foreword

I had a pretty tricky childhood. On reflection, it's amazing that I survived, let alone that I grew to thrive. For both the surviving and the thriving I owe a debt of gratitude to my school; a place where I was valued, loved, kept safe and stretched. So I write this foreword not in my role as an expert in the field, but in my role of a child who made it to adulthood thanks to people like you.

I'm writing this during the pandemic and I get overwhelmed with emotion when I think of the role that our schools and the everyday heroes within them have played in helping our children and communities find their way through. The role of the school has been growing for years to the delight of some and the horror of others; but the bigger, brighter, more brilliant role of schools as hearts of their communities and havens of safety even in the most difficult times will, I believe, be firmly cemented in the nation's conscience forever more.

This book is a real gift to the community of people who care for children in our schools. It provides the framework, practical actions and questions for exploration that will enable you to take your pastoral care to the next level as either an individual or as a whole team. Dip in and out and make it your own because no two schools are the same; but let Maria guide you as she has guided so many every day in her generosity of spirit, her willingness to embrace what works and learn from what doesn't, and her remarkable ability to get things done.

Imagine Maria by your side along with the thousands of others who, like you, put their students at the heart of their everyday and are always looking for ways to care more, to care better, to enable every student not just to survive but to thrive.

Following a training session I recently delivered about our role as the providers of pastoral care, I was challenged by a senior leader who said, 'We're here to teach them, not to love them.' I disagree. Love takes many forms and I believe that by teaching our children, keeping them safe and enabling them to reach for the stars we commit the ultimate acts of love…

… And this book is a roadmap to that love. Good luck with your travels and from the bottom of my heart, thank you to each and every one of you for caring.

Dr Pooky Knightsmith

1 An introduction to proactive pastoral care

Overview

This chapter will:

- define proactive pastoral care
- look at reactive and proactive pastoral care structures
- consider who should be responsible for proactive pastoral care
- discuss what proactive pastoral care involves.

It should be mentioned that the term 'pastoral care' is something that is unique to the British educational system, so our international colleagues often become confused and surprised, as the word 'pastoral' carries religious connotations for them: they imagine shepherds caring for their sheep in Christian religious communities. We can see how this could in some way contribute to the definition of pastoral care in education. However, as 'pastoral care' is such a big area of responsibility, there still exist many variations and differences in definitions even within the national communities.

When delivering training, I often ask colleagues to tell me what pastoral care means to them. Very often pastoral care is associated with reactive safeguarding, dealing with behaviour, issuing sanctions, attending safeguarding meetings and many more jobs that will fall into the same category. This reactive approach has been prioritised due to increased accountability and results, as well as budget constraints. While a necessary part of the pastoral role, a reactive approach alone will never bring about long-term and effective change in a school community, in terms of how pupils achieve academically and develop into well-rounded young adults, and in terms of their levels of happiness and wellbeing throughout their time at school. In order to achieve long-term change, we need to turn our attention to one of the forgotten and neglected elements of pastoral care: *proactive pastoral care*. Before we go any further, I am going to define how I view proactive pastoral care, which will be the starting point of this chapter and the book as a whole.

What is proactive pastoral care?

Proactive pastoral care is the essential element of pastoral structures that focuses on creating, embedding and nurturing a community's wellbeing culture. Proactive pastoral care is preventative in its nature and has many long-term benefits: strengthening community values, promoting character education (formally and informally), and embedding a successful pastoral curriculum just to name a few.

As pastoral leaders, we prioritise our daily tasks and it comes as no surprise that the reactive elements take priority due to their urgent nature. At the same time, if we don't develop our proactive pastoral provision, we end up in a reactive vicious circle and we struggle to make positive, long-lasting changes.

Having worked with many schools over the past few years with various pastoral structures, I have noticed that the two things that make pastoral structures strong are:

1. giving pastoral staff the status needed to be able to make an impact

2. providing the pastoral training that staff require to grow professionally.

This has become more evident and apt during the COVID-19 pandemic, when pastoral leaders have tried to create some sense of safety and security from a distance. Leading in times of crisis has made many leaders re-evaluate their priorities and look at their pastoral structures through a lens of newly acquired experience.

Pastoral structures

Traditionally, most pastoral structures look like this and are associated predominantly with a stepped approach to poor behaviour:

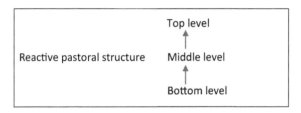

Tutors, pastoral administrative support staff, counsellors, nurses and so on are at the bottom level. The middle level consists of middle leaders – heads of year, heads of houses and heads of learning support. The top level includes senior leaders – the headteacher, deputy headteachers and assistant headteachers. If a pupil is misbehaving, the incident will be escalated in line with the pastoral structure: it could be a warning or a referral to the head of year after the agreed number of warnings. If someone has repeated their behaviour, some stages might be skipped in line with the school behaviour policy.

Proactive pastoral care functions the other way around. The main purpose of the proactive structure is not to punish, but to empower pastoral leaders at every stage to prevent the incident from happening in the first place or at least prevent it from escalating.

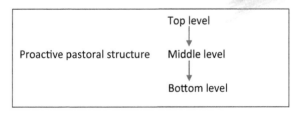

In my experience, these structures are working simultaneously in many education communities; however, the reactive structure is more developed, because it has to be due to compliancy requirements. Documents, such as behaviour, safeguarding and other pastoral policies, need regular updating in alignment with governmental updates and require consistent reactive implementation. However, in an ideal world, a school should get to the point where the proactive pastoral structure is *at least as* developed and prioritised as the reactive structure – if not more so. The overall pastoral structure should look like this:

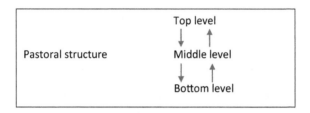

In order to give status and priority to proactive pastoral care, the top level should be occupied by staff who have the resources, knowledge and skills to establish and nurture a wellbeing culture; hence such responsibilities as pastoral curriculum and wellbeing should be held by someone who sits at the top level.

Let's consider the possible responsibilities of someone who has a wellbeing title. As we will establish in Chapter 3, page 41, wellbeing can be broken down into four separate areas: physical and mental health, emotional health, social health, and spiritual health. I am not suggesting that schools can be held responsible for the overall wellbeing of their pupils, but I am convinced that we can do a lot to support each area if we prioritise proactive pastoral care. However, we can only do so if it comes from the top level; hence the status plays an important role in the process. It is not possible to establish a wellbeing culture from the bottom. I have met a lot of colleagues who fought bit by bit to change their school culture, but ended with a number of wellbeing issues themselves. Their leaders used the word 'culture' to stifle innovation, to block wellbeing initiatives and to maintain the 'status quo'. This is the opposite of a wellbeing culture that promotes empowerment, ownership, initiative, empathy and growth. If we think about wellbeing as a garden, before we plant our trees or flowers, we need to prepare the soil by using a rake, breaking apart large clumps of soil, removing the roots and maybe even adding a fertiliser. By doing so, we are creating the most ideal growing situation. Bad soil can affect the development of roots, poor plant growth, and so on. It's the same with the school culture: if it's not right, wellbeing cannot be rooted in it.

Who should be responsible for proactive pastoral care?

It goes without saying that someone who holds the responsibility for proactive pastoral care needs to be involved in the long-term planning of school improvement and should have a big-picture overview of the school community. This will therefore be someone within the senior leadership team (SLT). If reactive pastoral care is 'short-term' care – for example, nurses or first-aiders dealing with a physical incident, or a head of year dealing with a friendship or bullying issue as it arises – proactive pastoral care is 'long term': it empowers young people to deal with various pastoral issues and feeds into our academic agenda. It could be ensuring that a pupil is able to pick the right GCSE, iGCSE or A level course, or it could be securing a variety of co-curricular opportunities to develop resilience, creativity, resourcefulness and reflection, and enabling young pupils to reconnect with their values and establish a strong moral compass.

During my work with pastoral leaders, it has become evident that one of the qualities that many value in a leader is emotional intelligence. We can think of many reasons why, but I am only going to dwell on one now. School communities consist of many groups – for example, SLT, heads of department, heads of year, Key Stage 3 and 4 teaching teams, A level teaching teams, working parties, and so on. Many staff would belong to various groups in line with their responsibilities. All of these groups are key to the success of delivering proactive pastoral care across a school. Someone who is responsible for proactive pastoral care needs to be able to engage with all these different groups, understand the emotional states of the groups and 'structure out destructive conflict'.

What does proactive pastoral care involve?

Educators Les Bell and Peter Maher (1986; quoted in Calvert and Henderson, 1998) identified four phases in the development of pastoral care:

Phase 1: With the expansion of comprehensive education in the late 1960s and early 1970s, the main goal was 'to control and discipline large numbers of pupils'.

Phase 2: This was followed by the development of care based on individual counselling, which proved problematic as it 'resulted in enormous demands on teacher time'.

Phase 3: Active tutor work (ATW) took place 'in isolation from the rest of the curriculum… reinforcing the idea of the separateness of pastoral activity'.

Phase 4: The final phase was a 'deliberate attempt to break down this artificial isolation of "caring" from the rest of school life'. During this phase, Michael Marland, headteacher and educationalist, became the first author to use the words 'pastoral care' in the title of his seminal book: *Pastoral Care* (1974).

Marland also proposed the term 'pastoral curriculum', arguing that this is 'a subset of the whole curriculum which deals with the development of the whole person' (Calvert and Henderson, 1998). In his book, Marland calls on educationalists not to see pastoral care 'merely as a way of supporting the academic work [but] looking after the total welfare of the pupil'. Marland quotes W. D. Wall when he says that pastoral care involves supporting a young person to construct various 'selves': the 'social, sexual, vocational and philosophic'. A school's academic curriculum contributes to the development of these selves, meaning that any attempt to draw a hard line dividing the pastoral and academic is artificial. If we take a holistic view of education and aim to develop a child as a 'whole person', 'good teaching, guidance and care are inextricable' and 'it is the pastoral task of the school which Marland sees as "central"' (Best, 2014).

The emphasis on control and discipline is still very much essential to reactive pastoral care. Despite the ever-changing context, many heads of year and their line managers (usually deputy headteachers) I have worked with over the years still spend most of their time dealing with behaviour incidents (which are becoming more complex, partly due to the development of social media platforms). However, if we consider schools to play a more holistic role in the development of young people in the four areas that Marland considers vital – the social, sexual, vocational and philosophic – proactive pastoral care must become a priority.

Proactive pastoral care that aims to develop these four selves will involve various different elements, but at the heart of each element is the concept of **wellbeing**. In the following chapters, I define my own four areas of health and wellbeing that I believe proactive pastoral care must consider – physical and mental health, emotional health, social health, and spiritual health. The ultimate aim of proactive pastoral care is to develop and support each of these areas to nurture learners to be happy, healthy and successful. I have identified three core elements of proactive pastoral care that are paramount to achieving this:

- **Character education:** The development of resilience, a well-developed moral compass and personal skills, in a manner that enables young people to remain mentally, physically, emotionally and socially healthy.
- **Parental engagement:** Engaging parents beyond them simply being interested in the academic progress of their child, and ensuring that pastoral engagement is a priority throughout a child's schooling, not just when things go wrong.

- **PSHE curriculum:** Directed time to challenge and promote personal development, to be resilient and independent, and to acquire knowledge to empower them to make the right choices in their personal and academic lives.

Some of the above elements, such as wellbeing and character education, have been buzzwords for some time. As with any buzzwords, there is a danger of losing the real meaning of these essential aspects of pastoral care and turning them into a tick-box exercise. In the sections that follow, we will look at each of these fundamental elements of proactive pastoral care in more detail and I will include practical ideas to help schools embed them in practice.

Reflections

1. Is your pastoral structure reactive or proactive?

2. How would you describe your school culture? Does it provide 'the most ideal growing situation'?

3. Do you have a member of staff who holds responsibility for wellbeing?

4. What are you already doing in terms of proactive pastoral care to support each of the wellbeing areas?

Physical and mental health	Emotional health	Social health	Spiritual health

5. What else could you do? What opportunities could you offer? Add them to the table using a different-coloured pen.

_____

_____

_____

2 What is wellbeing?

> **Overview**
>
> This chapter will:
>
> - explore the research around wellbeing
> - consider the various theories that inform how we think about wellbeing today
> - offer practical advice for starting a conversation around wellbeing among staff and pupils to support proactive pastoral care.

Wellbeing is something that is personal. Many people have attempted to define wellbeing in many different ways, which makes it rather illusive and hard to teach. Some would even go further than that and question whether it's possible to teach wellbeing in the same way as they would question teaching happiness. Using my knowledge and experience as a teacher, a researcher and a fellow human being with many personal roles and responsibilities, in this chapter I aim to provide you with some theoretical and practical wellbeing knowledge, giving ideas to implement in your classrooms and providing a reflection and strategic planning space for those who hold wellbeing responsibilities.

As we have established, wellbeing lies at the heart of proactive pastoral care. The core aim of pastoral care is to ensure the highest possible levels of wellbeing for pupils, both in terms of their experiences in school and also in their lives outside of school. Proactive pastoral care in particular should aspire to support pupils throughout their school years and set them up to lead healthy, happy and fulfilled lives beyond formal education too. In order to plan for and achieve this, it is paramount that educators have a secure grasp of what wellbeing means, and the theory and research behind wellbeing. In these sections, I therefore try to bridge the gap between research and practice, showing how you could enhance your pastoral practices by taking a reflective and research-based approach towards wellbeing. This chapter aims to help you as a pastoral leader to become fully aware of the debates and theories around wellbeing. There are also suggestions to help you ensure that fellow teachers have an understanding of them too, as they play a key role as subject teachers and form tutors in delivering your pastoral approach on a day-to-day basis. Furthermore, an essential element of proactive pastoral care involves teaching pupils about wellbeing: what it means, why it's important and how they can take care of their wellbeing throughout their lives. This chapter therefore also offers practical suggestions to help start these conversations in the classroom.

I have to apologise in advance: this chapter and the next are some of the longest chapters in the book, as wellbeing is the foundation of everything else that we discuss. However, I would advise reading all sections to ensure that you fully benefit from the content of the chapter.

Wellbeing theories

Wellbeing is a topic that has prompted a lot of debate. Is it possible to define wellbeing? Is it something that we have control over, or does our environment determine whether we can achieve the state of wellbeing? Does wellbeing mean different things to different people? I remember doing a literature review on wellbeing for my PhD research and feeling that I'd hit a brick wall, as most researchers were honest about the complexity of the subject and difficulties that arise as a result of various ways to approach it. I read the following:

- 'Wellbeing is a complex, multi-faceted construct that has continued to elude researchers' attempts to define and measure it.' (Pollard and Lee, 2003)

- 'Depending on the situation, scientists use different definitions of well-being and they use the term "well-being" to denote quite different things in different research projects… "well-being" refers to states of mind in psychology (happiness, satisfaction, or sense of flourishing), to satisfaction of preferences in economics, to objective quality of life in development contexts, to aspects of perceived or actual health in medical research, and so on.' (Alexandrova, 2017)

- 'The prospects of consensus seem remote, since there are a number of rival theories, and no obvious means of resolving the debate between them.' (Taylor, 2015)

During that time, I often questioned my eagerness to say 'yes' and my willingness to accept challenges, as well as the effect that my decision-making was having on my own wellbeing. However, I then came across one particular book and one particular sentence: 'The idea and the concept of wellbeing is manifold, widespread and goes historically back to ancient times.' (Glatzer, 2001) That was definitely one of the many eureka moments for me during that time. Why didn't I think before to go back in history and look at how the topic of wellbeing has been approached throughout the years by philosophers, researchers and our long-lost ancestors? As I absorbed the knowledge of many books, articles and observations, I was able to simplify and categorise different ideas and aspects related to this vast area. I have classified these ideas into subjective wellbeing theories, objective wellbeing theories and hybrid wellbeing theories.

Here is a diagram to summarise these three categories and the theories that I have used to create my own definition of wellbeing:

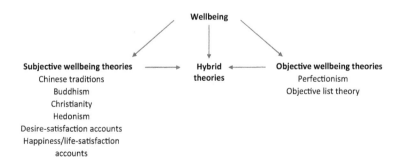

Wellbeing

Subjective wellbeing theories
Chinese traditions
Buddhism
Christianity
Hedonism
Desire-satisfaction accounts
Happiness/life-satisfaction accounts

Hybrid theories

Objective wellbeing theories
Perfectionism
Objective list theory

It must be emphasised that some uncertainty surrounding these theories remains, as 'not all theorists regard these categories as helpful and not all theories fit neatly into one or the other' (Taylor, 2012). Nevertheless, I found this classification useful when trying to break the topic of wellbeing down into manageable areas to work on. This famous phrase comes to mind: 'How do you eat an elephant? One bite at a time.' With every little research step forward, I started to gain knowledge and understanding. I would now like to present this to you in a simplified form.

Subjective and objective wellbeing

Before we look at each theory individually, I'd like to explain the difference between subjective and objective wellbeing. In simple terms, **subjective wellbeing** is concerned with some sort of internal phenomena or characteristics like happiness, pleasure or desire, while **objective wellbeing** focuses on the objective components of life, for example material resources or some sort of social attributes such as education or connections.

All the subjective and objective theories listed in the diagram have differences and variations depending on their origin and how and by whom the original theory was developed. Without going into much detail, I will now give a brief overview of the aforementioned theories and how they relate to our current wellbeing practices in schools.

Subjective wellbeing theories

We will begin by looking at the subjective wellbeing theories.

Chinese traditions

Defeng Yang and Han Zhou (2017), academics at Jinan University in Guangzhou, consider the differences in how wellbeing is understood in Chinese and Western cultures. They say, 'Traditionally in Chinese culture, well-being isn't defined specifically but expressed using the word "Le" (happiness), "Le" is a psychological experience which is based on an empirical, inner experience of feelings.' When Yang and Zhou consider wellbeing from the point of view of Taoism, an ancient religious and philosophical tradition that is deeply rooted in Chinese customs and worldview, they note that 'Taoism's view of happiness requires people to look beyond reality for happiness and suggests that happiness could be acquired from appreciating the beauty of nature and life.' It promotes a simple and selfless life in harmony with the 'Dao' (the way of nature) and distinguishes between natural and acquired desires. Justin Tiwald (2017) of San Francisco State University defines the former as desires that 'arise spontaneously from ourselves' and the latter as 'desires that come about because of the novel effects of external things, whether those things be material objects or living creatures'. Tiwald explains the dangers of acquired desires, in that they 'are usually to the detriment of the desirer's well-being; satisfying them has little inherent value and pursuing them tends to lead to greater frustration and conflict.'

Nowadays, we can witness many attempts in the UK to show the importance of nature for our wellbeing, and having access to the outside world is considered an essential component of wellbeing. For example, the World Wildlife Fund, the world's leading independent conservation organisation, and the Mental Health Foundation have recently produced a guide titled *Thriving with Nature*. The director for England and Wales at the Mental Health Foundation, Dr Antonis Kousoulis, stated, 'Growing evidence suggests that being in nature has a very positive effect on our mental health, providing protective and restorative benefits.' (Mental Health Foundation, 2020) Such is the importance of nature for wellbeing that Kousoulis called for any new housing developments and public spaces being built to take into consideration the importance of everyone having access to a park, garden, lake or other natural space. He also drew connections between environmental damage and mental health, saying, 'We need to get serious about cherishing the natural world and acknowledge that human thriving depends on it.' The guide provides readers with information about wellbeing and offers wellbeing activities according to the four seasons. It is available to download for free on the Mental Health Foundation website.

Buddhism

In Buddhism, wellbeing is discussed in three different ways. Christopher Gowans (2015) at Fordham University describes them as follows:

1. According to the doctrines of karma and rebirth, the moral quality of a person's life causally influences the person's future wellbeing in their present or consequent lives.

2. All lives in the cycle of rebirth are deficient in wellbeing to some considerable extent because they involve suffering, but it is possible to overcome this suffering by escaping the cycle of rebirth through the attainment of enlightenment.

3. Fundamental Buddhist virtues such as compassion and loving kindness involve a concern to promote the wellbeing of other people.

Mindfulness meditation aims to train a person's attention towards the present moment, while loving-kindness meditation aims to channel warm, positive, compassionate emotions and feelings towards oneself and other people – starting with those closest to you and extending to all people and creatures on Earth. Mindfulness and loving-kindness meditations both emerged from ancient Buddhist mind-training practices, and are now being used by many educational establishments to enhance the wellbeing of staff and pupils. In 2019, the Anna Freud National Centre for Children and Families, in partnership with University College London, launched an initiative to introduce mindfulness to 370 schools in England in an effort to teach pupils to look after their mental health. The initiative is being run as a trial until 2021 and the government hopes that it will provide information regarding which mental health practices can benefit students in schools. It's well worth keeping an eye out for any findings.

Many people consider mindfulness to be particularly important in the current age of digital technology: 'Nowadays, within the overloaded world of information, we are always "online". In other words, we are *mind-full*: our mind continuously collects endless information consciously or/and unconsciously.' (Tang, 2017) As our minds are constantly receiving and processing information, we do not have the capacity to reorganise or digest all the information being thrown at us. The benefits of mindfulness are much lauded. In his foreword to the book *Mindfulness* by Mark Williams and Danny Penman (2011), Jon Kabat-Zinn, the founder of Mindfulness-Based Stress Reduction, claims that 'the practice of mindfulness has been shown to exert a powerful influence on one's health, well-being and happiness'. The authors Williams and Penman themselves claim that mindfulness 'can prevent normal feelings of anxiety, stress and sadness from spiralling downwards into prolonged periods of unhappiness and exhaustion – or even serious clinical depression'. However, it is fair to say that mindfulness must be a regular practice in order for its full benefits to be felt. Kabat-Zinn says, 'its cultivation is a process, one that of necessity unfolds and deepens over time.'

In support of loving-meditation practice, Barbara Fredrickson (2008), in her article 'Promoting positive affect', introduces the broaden-and-build theory, claiming that negative emotions narrow people's ideas about possible actions while positive emotions broaden them. She cites a number of studies before coming to the conclusion that 'practising loving-kindness meditation reliably augmented people's daily experiences of positive emotions, and those increases in positive emotions, in turn, accounted for gains in a wide range of personal resources, ranging from sleep quality to resilience and mindfulness. These resources gains, in turn, elevated signs of flourishing mental health.'

However, despite these positive findings, Tang (2017) advises us to be cautious and warns that 'although a number of cross-sectional studies suggested positive changes associated with meditation, this design precludes causal attribution: it is possible that there are pre-existing differences in the brains of meditators, which might be linked to their interest in meditation, motivation, expectancy, personality, and other factors.' When thinking about introducing mindfulness into the classroom, we should question the commitment and self-discipline of pupils and have realistic expectations regarding its effect on wellbeing. We might just be planting a seed: something that our young people might come back to in time.

Christianity

In terms of Christianity, Fontana (2011) suggests that it 'emphasizes something that too often becomes overlooked, namely the importance of conscience, of a sense that one should do what is right because it is right, not because others are looking on or there is a risk of being caught out in wrong-doing or even that there is the chance of praise or reward for good behaviour'.

A number of researchers have observed a decline in Christianity in recent years. For example, the author Paul Silas Peterson (2017) claims that 'the situation that is emerging in most of the Western world... is the formation of a diverse field of various competing religious communities and worldviews within the broader context of secularization.' This idea is echoed by Charles Taylor (1991) when he talks about 'malaises of modernity... features of our contemporary culture and society that people experience as a loss or a decline, even as our civilization "develops"'. The author argues that our modern life is characterised by 'loss of meaning, the fading of moral horizons'.

The Revd Canon Professor Leslie J. Francis from the University of Warwick has done a lot of research in the area. He has designed The Francis Scale of Attitude towards Christianity for use among young people between the ages of eight and 16 years (Francis, 1978). A series of studies in a variety of cultural contexts found a positive correlation between religious affect and happiness. One project you might consider for your school is Understanding Christianity, as it integrates pupils' understanding of theological concepts with their own self-understanding and understanding of the world.

Hedonism and desire-satisfaction theory

The ethical theory of hedonism has a long history, stretching back to ancient Greece. Ethical hedonism claims that pleasure, and the absence of pain, is the *summum bonum*, the only thing of value in its own right, and that other things have value only indirectly, in so far as they produce pleasure or remove pain (Taylor, 2012). Put simply, the main goal of a hedonistic lifestyle is to relentlessly pursue pleasure and satisfaction.

Desire-satisfaction theory (also known as desire-fulfilment theory, preferentism or desire theory) was rejected by many ancient and medieval philosophers (Heathwood, 2017), but has become one of the most popular theories nowadays. According to the theory, 'what is intrinsically valuable for a person must have a connection with what [they] would find in some degree compelling or attractive' (Railton, 1986). In other words, your life will be going well for you as long as you get what you desire.

I have seen these theories used for a class debate. The question was: 'Do you agree with the following statement? When someone wants something to be the case and it is, or becomes, the case, this is a benefit to the person.' The responses and scenarios suggested by pupils demonstrated a great deal of self-awareness and critical thinking.

Happiness/life-satisfaction accounts

According to happiness/life-satisfaction accounts, welfare 'consists in authentic happiness. This theory is subjective, since it makes a subject's welfare depend on her attitudes' (Sumner, 1996). Conversely, if the happiness of an individual is based on values that are not their own, their happiness becomes 'inauthentic'. Many researchers would argue that the value of authenticity is the foundation of wellbeing. For example, according to Wood et al. (2008), in mainstream counselling psychology, authenticity is viewed as the most fundamental aspect of wellbeing, in that it is not just a component or prerequisite to achieving wellbeing but it is the very essence of wellbeing. While a lack of authenticity can lead to psychopathology and distress because it causes people to engage in forced, unnatural behaviour, leaving them feeling unfulfilled or devalued (Leary, 2004), it is believed that promoting authenticity may lead to enhanced wellbeing because it helps people have a clear and consistent sense of self, causing fulfilment (Rogers, 1961).

The most obvious question at this stage would be: 'But what is authenticity?' If you were to search for 'authenticity' online, you would find a variety of books, articles, TED Talks and blogs telling us how to be true to ourselves. I would define the word 'authentic' as being aware of all parts of the self – emotions, traits, strengths, weaknesses, desires, motives, and so on, being honest with oneself and accepting parts of the self that might conflict and contradict each other, as well as behaving with integrity and in alignment with one's core values. Schools play a vital role in nurturing a culture of authenticity and empowering staff and pupils to be self-aware and true to themselves, act with confidence and feel that they belong. To do this, schools must 'cultivate the courage to be imperfect – and vulnerable' and make staff and pupils feel they are 'fundamentally worthy of love and acceptance, just as [they] are' (Brown, 2010).

Objective wellbeing

In the same way as subjective theories, objective theories are similar to each other in nature but also present us with a number of variations. For example, while objective list theories claim that a number of goods contribute to a person's wellbeing, perfectionist theories hold that what items on the list have in common is their contribution to the realisation of human nature.

Objective list theories maintain that if we possess all or most of a certain list of 'goods', then we can attain wellbeing. Here are some of those 'lists of goods' according to proponents of this theory:

Finnis's list	Fletcher's list	Griffin's list
• Life • Knowledge • Play • Aesthetic experience • Friendship • Religion • Practical reasonableness	• Achievement • Friendship • Happiness • Pleasure • Self-respect • Virtue	• Accomplishment • The components of human existence (e.g. autonomy and liberty) • Understanding • Enjoyment ('the perception of beauty') • Deep personal relations

Gomez-Lobo's list	Murphy's list	Parfit's list
• Life • Family, friendship • Work and play • Aesthetic experience • Knowledge and integrity	• Life • Knowledge • Aesthetic experience • Excellence in play and at work • Excellence in agency • Inner peace • Friendship and community • Religion • Happiness	• Moral goodness • Rational activity • Development of abilities • Having children and being a good parent • Knowledge • Awareness of true beauty

We can observe some differences in the lists, but we can also see many similarities. Achievement, accomplishment, work, excellence at work and development of abilities are closely connected. Friendship, personal relationships, community, having children and being a good parent highlight the need for healthy personal relationships.

All the goods on the lists look reasonable, although you might have already picked your favourite list or added something that is important to you to one of the existing lists. However, the main restriction of the objective list theory is that it does not give a 'fundamental role to people's beliefs about what is good for them'. Thus, we are not free, according to the objective list theories, to 'devise our own lists, so to speak'. An objective list theorist believes that the items on the list encompass everything that is good for all humans and that these items are the only things that are good for everyone (Fletcher, 2016). This makes the theory quite restrictive.

I have seen a number of activities around the lists incorporated in tutor time, assemblies and PSHE. Usually they are centred around identifying priorities and managing time to ensure we do not neglect important areas of our lives. One activity could be the Wheel of Life, used in coaching as a visual tool to identify how balanced your life is.

Wellbeing theories: a summary

We have now covered a number of subjective and objective theories. To simplify them even further, I am going to present them in a way that could be used as a handy reference and a reminder of what each of them represents.

Wellbeing

Subjective wellbeing	**Objective wellbeing**
Moral requirements	Objective requirements
Intrinsic value	
	Objective list theories
Chinese traditions	Objective goods you must have
'Le' (happiness)	
Values	**Perfectionism**
Ethics	Objective goods that contribute to perfect
Sage within	human life
Buddhism	
Moral life	
Enlightenment	
Compassion	
Loving kindness	
Christianity	
Relationship with God/Faith/Spirit	
Hedonism	
Pleasure	
Desire-satisfaction accounts	
Importance of desires	
Happiness/life-satisfaction accounts	
Authentic happiness	

As you can see, there are quite obvious differences between subjective and objective theories, but it comes as no surprise that some researchers believe that wellbeing can be both subjective and objective, hence **hybrid theories** of wellbeing have been put forward. They have become quite attractive to many because of their dual nature. Some contemporary philosophers even suggest that hybrid theories of wellbeing are among the most popular theories nowadays. It is quite natural that most of us would desire some basic goods on the list; however, it might be that we do not desire them in the same way or to the same extent depending on our inner make-up. For example, an introvert might desire friendship in its purest internal sense – trust, honesty, support – but might reject the external factors that come with it: change of routine, lack of time and possible break of trust. Hybrid theories allow us to look at wellbeing from different angles. As Haybron (2008) puts it, hybrid theories of wellbeing remain popular as their chief appeal is their inclusiveness: 'All the components of subjective well-being seem important, and there is probably no component of subjective well-being that does not, at times, get included in happiness in ordinary usage.'

Modern wellbeing theories

In their book *Subjective Well-being: Measuring happiness, suffering, and other dimensions of experience*, Arthur Stone and Christopher Mackie (2013) divide subjective wellbeing into two categories: evaluative and experienced. They define the categories as follows:

- **Evaluative wellbeing:** This involves 'judgments of how satisfying one's life is'. These judgements could be applied to various aspects of life, including relationships, community, health and work.

- **Experienced wellbeing:** This relates to people's emotional states, taking into account factors such as physical sensations (perhaps pain or arousal) and emotional sensations (perhaps purpose or pointlessness). Experienced wellbeing can be divided into positive experiences and negative experiences. The former could be characterised as joy, contentment and happiness, and the latter as sadness, stress, worry, pain and suffering.

Many modern theories take a holistic approach to wellbeing, considering various different aspects and how they interrelate. For example, Rath and Harter (2010) distinguish between career, social, financial and physical wellbeing. Yarcheski et al. (1994) consider mental, psychological, physical and social dimensions. Hausman (2015) defines wellbeing as 'flourishing', explaining that this 'depends on how the things that make human lives good (such as friendship, happiness, health or a sense of purpose) are integrated into the dynamic structure of that individual's life' – in other words, 'the dynamic coherent integrations of objective goods into an identity.'

The 2004 report by the Department for Education and Skills, 'Promoting emotional health and well-being through the national healthy school standard', defined emotional health and wellbeing as 'a holistic, subjective state which is present when a range of feelings, among them energy, confidence, openness, enjoyment, happiness, calm, and caring are combined and balanced'. Dodge et al. (2012) propose the following definition:'Stable wellbeing is when individuals have the psychological, social and physical resources they need to meet a particular psychological, social and/or physical challenge. When individuals have more challenges than resources, the see-saw dips, along with their wellbeing, and vice-versa.' At this point, it is important to highlight that health has often been approached from a point of view of 'absence of pathology and suffering' (Elmer et al., 2003). However, Pollard and Lee (2003) also express a concern with this definition in that 'well-being is often framed within a model of child deficits rather than a model of child strengths'. This may mean that wellbeing research, policy and practice focus too much on children's deficits, rather than the possibility of identifying and promoting children's strengths.

Although transpersonal wellbeing is often neglected in the school curriculum, it is a very important area to consider, as it deals extensively with matters relating to human values and spiritual experience. When we talk about transpersonal wellbeing, we may focus on inner peace, harmony, pursuit of meaning even in difficult times, or personal growth. We look inwards, rather than outwards. To empower us to create a meaningful life and reconnect with ourselves, transpersonal therapists use a number of tools, such as mindful meditation, art, journaling, music, breathing exercises, yoga and visualisation. I have seen many of these being used at schools and recommended to pupils to practise outside of school to help them manage periods of anxiety and stress.

*

So far, we have looked at subjective, objective, hybrid and modern theories of wellbeing. This provides a solid foundation as we attempt to create a more concrete model of wellbeing in relation to pastoral care in Chapter 3. But before we go any further, how can we put what we have discovered into practice and share it with staff and pupils?

Sharing wellbeing theories with staff

Very often, wellbeing CPD sessions attract negative attention and reactions; this is due to the fact that we are trying to spoon-feed staff without explaining the complexity of the topic or empowering them to make decisions regarding their own wellbeing. In order for wellbeing sessions to bring benefit to staff and to the pupils they are going to teach, it is important to dig deeper: we should aim to explain various approaches towards wellbeing and give staff safe space to nurture self-awareness. It might be tempting to tick wellbeing boxes by making staff go to yoga, mindfulness, art, singing or any other 'wellbeing' sessions, and encouraging them to run these sessions with pupils, but the truth is they are only going to be beneficial if staff conscientiously make a decision to attend them and use them in the classroom based on their knowledge and awareness of their own needs and those of pupils. In every wellbeing session I deliver, I emphasise the importance of following these three steps:

The information I have presented so far will have given you sufficient basic theoretical knowledge to understand the complexity of the topic of wellbeing. As it is one of the most debated topics stretching across various disciplines, it is possible to spend hours and hours researching different approaches and theories, which for me has been extremely fascinating, but also extremely time-consuming. The history of wellbeing plays an important role not only in educating ourselves, but also in getting other adults on board. Wellbeing is not a wishy-washy, 'soft' subject that has suddenly become popular; it is a very complex and challenging research area.

In a wellbeing session with staff, you could share the basic theoretical knowledge offered above and then offer some thinking time for participants:

1. What theories appeal to you? Why?

2. What theories do you disagree with? Why?

3. If you had to choose one of the theories discussed, which one would it be? Why?

4. How would it enrich or change your life?

These questions can be asked during an 'introduction to wellbeing' session and are designed to get staff thinking and increasing their self-awareness. We often find ourselves stuck on the express train that life is without paying enough attention to ourselves and our needs, and we develop a self-awareness glitch that hinders our wellbeing, so reflection time should be an essential component of any wellbeing training.

It is also important not just to have theoretical knowledge of self-awareness, but also to obtain something that I would call practical knowledge. Recently, personality profiling has been used by many individuals and organisations for a variety of reasons. I often use it to enhance self-awareness and to build up practical knowledge. You might have already come across tools like the Myers-Briggs Type Indicator® (MBTI®) personality inventory, the DiSC (dominance, influence, conscientiousness, steadiness) assessment, the VIA Character Strengths survey or the 16 Personality Factor Questionnaire. If you haven't used these tools before, I would recommend using them as they can enhance self-awareness and prompt further conversations. They are also great hands-on activities for any wellbeing training as they bring an interactive element to the session.

Theories related to human needs

Following on from there, you could also look at a couple of theories that need to be mentioned in relation to human needs. The first one is the well-known Maslow's Hierarchy of Needs (1943). According to the theory, there are five levels of human needs, and they are usually displayed as a pyramid:

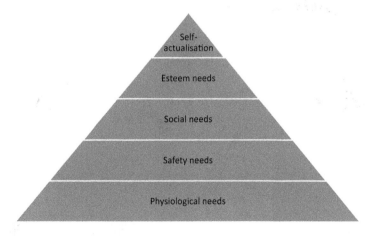

Self-actualisation

Esteem needs

Social needs

Safety needs

Physiological needs

The **lowest** level is our **physiological** needs (our need for food, warmth, sleep, air and so on). If these needs are not met, our bodies will struggle to function.

The **fourth** level is our **safety** level. Our need for shelter, employment security, law and order can be found on this level.

The **third** level – **social needs** – highlights the importance of family, friendship and intimacy.

The **second** level – **esteem** needs – incorporates our needs for confidence, recognition, status and respect.

The **highest** level is **self-actualisation**, which focuses on realising an individual's potential, such as growth, fulfilment and creativity.

As Maslow (1968) says, 'It is quite true that man lives by bread alone – when there is no bread. But what happens to man's desires when there is plenty of bread and when his belly is chronically filled? At once other (and "higher") needs emerge and these, rather than physiological hungers, dominate the organism. And when these in turn are satisfied, again new (and still "higher") needs emerge and so on. This is what we mean by saying that the basic human needs are organized into a hierarchy of relative prepotency.' This theory is a great reminder to teachers and leaders that we are all unique and might find ourselves at different levels of the hierarchy due to our external circumstances – as might the pupils we work with. We can be motivated by different things, and need to be rewarded and praised in different ways – and again, this is the case for pupils too. You can earn good money and still lack fulfilment if other needs are not met, which means that our wellbeing will suffer as a result.

The second theory is McClelland's Acquired Needs Theory. McClelland built on Maslow's work and in his 1961 book, *The Achieving Society*, distinguished between three main needs: achievement, affiliation and power (influence). According to Richard Daft (2008), 'the acquired needs theory proposes that certain types of needs are acquired during an individual's lifetime. In other words, people are not born with those needs but may learn them through their life experiences.' Irrespective of age, gender, ethnicity, and so on, we all have three motivating drivers, and one of those drivers will be our dominant driver. The use of the theory in practice can significantly increase self-awareness. One note of caution from experience: I wasn't entirely honest with myself when I was going through this for the first time, as I didn't want to come across as needing power. I felt much more comfortable using the word 'influence', as it has many more positive connotations for me. This in itself increased my self-awareness, as it made me reflect about why I had a problem with the word 'power'.

*

Personality profiling, needs and motivation theories are just a few examples of how you can support staff in gaining self-awareness during your wellbeing training. As you come to know your staff better, look at what would work for them and design your sessions with that knowledge in mind.

School culture

While developing knowledge and self-awareness require the active involvement of staff in the process, the last action step is slightly different. It would be impossible for staff to put their newly acquired knowledge into action if the school did not provide the right conditions. The school culture is determined by school leaders, by the headteacher, their vision and the ethos and values of the school.

How can staff take positive action for both themselves and their pupils if they are overwhelmed by high demands in terms of marking, observations, report-writing and meetings? How can they take positive action if the relationships between colleagues are poor, if unhealthy competition is encouraged between departments or if staff are being bullied? If staff are not able to take positive action, that means that their wellbeing cannot be embedded in the school culture. So, let's take a moment to reflect on the following questions:

1. How can your school enable staff to take action to improve wellbeing across the school?
2. What changes need to be made or what further changes can be made?

3. Whose responsibility is it to make those changes? By when?

4. How and how often will progress be monitored?

5. Is this reflected in the school wellbeing development plan?

In my experience, using the three-step approach, knowledge – self-awareness – practice, gives communities a secure framework to work with. Each community is unique as we are unique as individuals, and you might find that different ways of introducing knowledge, increasing self-awareness or creating conditions for positive action might work, but you need to go up the steps in that particular order for the sustainable changes to be made. This process of staff wellbeing training should be at the heart of your proactive pastoral care provision. Once teachers have a secure grasp of the theory and research behind wellbeing, have gained a level of self-awareness and understand how to put this into practice, they are then ready to share and work on this with pupils.

Sharing wellbeing theories with pupils

We are now going to look at different ways to transfer our knowledge into practice in a classroom with young people. You can share these ideas with teachers as part of your staff training sessions to help them initiate discussions about wellbeing in their classrooms and ensure pupils begin to grasp the importance of wellbeing and what they can do to take better care of themselves during their school years and beyond.

When introducing pupils to the topic of wellbeing, it's important to follow the same process as with staff: knowledge – self-awareness – practice. It is well worth beginning with a brief session on the history of wellbeing to share the central theories. This could be adapted from the necessary information in the research sections above. Following this session, discussions, debates and reflections could be quite interesting. Not only will pupils be getting an opportunity to think and increase their self-awareness, but you will also be able to find out more about them, what drives them or what challenges them. You could have a go at the following tasks:

- **Debating tasks:** Do you think wellbeing is cultivated within ourselves (subjective wellbeing) or is it shaped by our environment (objective wellbeing)?
- **Thinking tasks:** What is important for your wellbeing? Do you think the same would apply to everybody? Why or why not?
- **Reflection tasks:** Let's have a look at the list of 'goods' that are essential to our wellbeing according to Alfonso Gómez-Lobo, a professor of metaphysics and moral philosophy:
  - *family*
  - *friendship*
  - *work and play*
  - *aesthetic experience*
  - *knowledge*
  - *integrity.*

Would you add or remove any of these 'goods'? What would your list look like?

In the next chapter I will be introducing a four-part wellbeing model that will give you further ideas for talking about wellbeing with pupils.

Reflections

Staff:

1. What would you like staff to know about wellbeing?

_____

_____

_____

2. How could they receive that knowledge?

_____

_____

_____

3. How could they use that knowledge to enhance the
   pastoral care provision in your school?

_____

_____

_____

4. What would be the benefits of staff using that knowledge
   in terms of pastoral care?

_____

_____

_____

Pupils:

1. What knowledge do pupils need to have?

_____

_____

_____

2. How could they receive that knowledge?

_____

_____

_____

3. Which activities are you and your staff going to try?

_____

_____

_____

4. When are you going to try them?

_____

_____

_____

3 A four-part wellbeing model for pastoral care

Overview

This chapter will:

- consider the language we use to talk about wellbeing
- offer practical suggestions for encouraging and supporting pupils to talk about wellbeing with confidence
- provide a four-part model for wellbeing that can be used as a basis for planning proactive pastoral care in schools
- offer a practical activity to introduce this model to pupils.

It will come as no surprise that the language currently being used around wellbeing is vast with many nuances and uncertainties. There are many different possible definitions of wellbeing and this also varies between cultures. The language we use when we talk about wellbeing is crucial to our understanding of our own wellbeing and how we can take care of it. In this chapter I am going to consider several definitions of wellbeing that are currently in existence and how we talk about wellbeing, before offering my own four-part model for wellbeing that can be used as a basis for how we approach proactive pastoral care in schools.

The language of wellbeing

We are going to have a look at how wellbeing can be defined in different cultures, as well as how language can contribute to our wellbeing. The language of wellbeing has been at the centre of the debate as it often reflects cultural understanding of wellbeing. According to the Norwegian researchers Carlquist et al. (2017), 'Although phenomena of living well are conceptualized in most – if not all – cultures worldwide, considerable variation has been detected in *how* people conceptualize and think about well-being.'

Nowadays, the term 'wellbeing' exists in many different languages: in French, it is known as 'bien-être' and in Spanish as 'bien estar'. In German, the words 'Wohlbefinden' and 'Wohlfahrt' are closely related to wellbeing and have their roots in 'wol varn', a term in the medieval German language that means 'live happy' (Glatzer, 2001). However, wellbeing is much more complex than simply living 'happily' or living 'well' as these Western terms might suggest. Daniel Haybron (2008), a professor of philosophy, in fact says that in order to experience wellbeing in the full sense of the word, 'people everywhere need to feel that their lives are worth living'. He concedes that this is difficult to express in most languages 'because there is no term for it', but points to the Japanese language, which has a word to sum it up perfectly: *ikigai*. Haybron defines this term as meaning 'that which most makes one's life worth living', and specifies that this could be related to work, family, a specific dream or religion. For Haybron, this notion transcends culture, language and society. He says, 'once we moved beyond the barrier of language – the lack of a term like *ikigai* in languages other than Japanese – the same is the case for people in societies beyond Japan.' Although we often use the phrase 'the good life' when we talk about wellbeing, it is important to bear in mind that this term can mean different things, as we can interpret the word 'good' in different ways, which do not necessarily convey the meaning of it being healthy for the individual.

Talking about wellbeing

The author Anna Alexandrova (2017) points out that 'In English, as in several other languages, the term "well-being" itself is rarely used in everyday life.' We hardly ever hear people say, 'How is your wellbeing?'

or 'My wellbeing has been good lately.' Instead, we invoke wellbeing using questions such as 'How are you doing?', 'How have you been?' or 'How is it going?' and in replies such as 'I am doing really well' or 'I am fine lately' or 'Average'. Of course, sometimes these questions are deployed as greetings rather than genuine questions. In the USA in particular, 'How are you doing?' is a greeting only and no reply is expected. Alexandrova points to Joey's chat-up line, 'How YOU doin'?', in the sitcom *Friends* as an example of this. Another researcher, Marc Brackett (2019), also states that we overuse the questions like 'How are you?', 'How are you doing?' and even 'How are you feeling?' In the same way that we overuse the questions we also overuse the answers: 'Great', 'Fine', 'OK'. We often ask the question out of habit or politeness and reply on autopilot without giving it a second thought. Brackett calls it 'one of the great paradoxes of the human condition – we ask some variation of the question "How are you feeling?" over and over, which would lead one to assume that we attach some importance to it. And yet we never expect or desire – or provide – an honest answer.' One of the acronyms I use with my pupils in class to highlight this phenomenon is F.I.N.E. – Feelings I'm Not Expressing.

Cultural phenomena aside, expressing our emotions and how we are feeling can be difficult. Dr Harry Barry (2018), author of *Emotional Resilience*, claims that 'we are often unsure as to how we feel. There are many reasons for this difficulty. Although emotions rule our lives, we often feel strangely uncomfortable reflecting on or discussing them. Men, especially, struggle to identify or accept their emotions.' This could be due to the stereotypes and expectations imposed by society: being emotional can be regarded as not holding it together and failing as a man. Brackett (2019) also notes that this can be a problem of vocabulary: not having the words to describe our feelings in detail. He states that when he talks to a group about how they are feeling, 'three-quarters of the people have a hard time coming up with a "feeling" word. When the words do come, they don't usually tell us very much. People fumble around a bit, hem and haw, and then use the most commonplace terms we all rely on – *I feel fine, good, okay.*'

It is much easier to describe how you feel physically than emotionally, and when we talk about how we feel physically, we feel less of a need to justify, scrutinise and evaluate our feelings. As Robert Solomon (1976) notes, 'We often say of our emotions that they are "reasonable" and "unreasonable", "warranted" and "unwarranted", "justifiable" and "unjustifiable", "legitimate" and "illegitimate", "sensible" and "foolish", "self-demeaning" and "enhancing", and even "right" and "wrong". Yet no such evaluations are appropriate in the realm of headaches and bellyaches, warm flushes and nausea.'

Another issue to note in relation to wellbeing vocabulary is that 'studies have shown that there is a greater variety of terms referring to negative emotions, as compared to positive emotions' (Schrauf and Sanchez, 2004). Green (1992) points out that 'It has often been remarked that negative emotions are more richly differentiated than positive emotions. The list is long on the side of anger, dread, envy, fear, grief, hatred, indignation, pity, remorse, and resentment; on the side of gladness, hope, joy, love, and pleasure, the list is short.' Wundt (1896/1897, cited in Averill, 1980) echoes this idea and explains: 'Obviously language has provided a much greater variety of names for unpleasurable emotions than for pleasurable. In fact, observation renders it probable that unpleasurable emotions exhibit a greater variety of forms of occurrence and that their different forms are really more numerous.' This could be due to the fact that as humans we are wired for survival, as early men were faced with many dangers that they had to overcome.

An interesting study of wellbeing language was conducted in Norway by the researchers Carlquist et al. (2017). They analysed how a number of evaluative words related to wellbeing have been used in the Norwegian media over the past two decades. The terms they included were as follows: *contented*; *positive thoughts* or *think positive*; *satisfied*; *satisfaction*; and *satisfied with life* or *life satisfaction*. They also added the broader expressions *good life* and *quality of life*, plus the literal Norwegian translation of *wellbeing* (*velvære*). They explained, 'In contrast to English, the Norwegian word has particular connotations of bodily pleasure and pampering.' Having analysed the data, the researchers observed that 'certain words, particularly *mastery, [motivation]* and *self-development*, have been rapidly taken up in Norwegian print media, suggesting that these words might serve particular ideological functions.' The frequency of other common words, such as *satisfied* and *satisfaction*, gradually decreased. This evidence shows that the language of wellbeing is constantly in flux, meaning how we perceive and talk about wellbeing as a society is incredibly complex and ever-changing. This in turn has an impact on how we think about our own wellbeing. It would be interesting to see what wellbeing language is being used in the British press and how it has changed over time to reflect the changes in our understanding or perceptions of wellbeing. If we were to take away anything from this research, it is that we should be mindful of what language we use when talking about wellbeing with our colleagues and pupils, and how we use this language in our day-to-day interactions.

Research into action: wellbeing language

It is really important that language used by staff and pupils around wellbeing is understood and consistent across a school. I find that using values-related language often helps to bridge the gap between the academic and the pastoral sides of school life. You might like to think about the following questions as a staff team as you consider what language you would like to use to talk about wellbeing:

- What can we do as a community to further expand and embed wellbeing vocabulary?
- How can we ensure consistency across the school?
- Are support staff aware of what we are doing? Do they require further training?
- How could wellbeing language further promote and underpin our wellbeing culture?

Something that is well worth doing is discussing the language of wellbeing with pupils to help them begin to consider some of the complex issues raised in the research in the previous section. Here is a task that you can include in tutor time or as part of a small-group discussion or a PSHE lesson to begin opening up the conversation about wellbeing language and embedding a consistent vocabulary across the school.

Explain to the pupils that in English, we would not ask a direct question like 'How is your wellbeing?' We often instead ask simply, 'How are you?' However, there are problems with this as a question if you're truly trying to ascertain someone's level of wellbeing and show that you care. Share some of the ideas in the research discussed in the previous section about this question being seen as a greeting rather than a genuine question that requires a response, and how easy it is to answer the question reflexively without pausing to think. So, what other questions can we come up with together to show somebody that we care about their wellbeing? Give pupils time to come up with some alternative questions, perhaps in groups or pairs, and then help guide a whole-class conversation.

Now ask the pupils to think about how they answer wellbeing questions by reflecting on the following:

- Do they think people are honest when it comes to answering questions like 'How are you?'?

- Do we really expect a truthful, detailed answer when we ask this?

- Why do pupils think people might not give an honest answer?

- What could we do to encourage them to be honest?

- What would non-judgemental language look like when we are talking about wellbeing in general or emotions in particular?

You could use books for storytelling and promoting the use of language to describe feelings and emotions. With secondary-age pupils, you could use photos. Describe the photo and then move onto how those people might be feeling in that moment. Choose photos where people display similar and different emotions to increase the complexity. You could also look at values, for example empathy and sympathy, and the difference between them.

A four-part model for wellbeing

Having analysed various wellbeing theories, both established and current, and having considered the language of wellbeing and how we might begin to discuss it with staff and pupils, I would now like to propose a hybrid wellbeing model that incorporates features present across various theories. I would also like to use the term 'authentic' to define wellbeing in order to highlight its subjective nature – by authentic, I mean true for the individual in question. I propose to bring to the forefront the following elements of wellbeing:

1. physical and mental health

2. family and social relations

3. emotions and mood

4. spiritual and moral goodness.

This four-part wellbeing model forms a solid basis for planning and implementing proactive pastoral care. An in-depth understanding of each category and how it can be nurtured through our pastoral structures, interventions and curriculum is essential for pastoral leaders. Let's look at each category in more detail.

1. Physical and mental health

'Men ought to know that from the brain and from the brain only arise our pleasures, joys, laughter, and jests as well as our sorrows, pains, griefs and tears… It is the same thing which makes us mad or delirious, inspires us with dread and fear, whether by night or by day, brings us sleeplessness, inopportune mistakes, aimless anxieties, absent-mindedness and acts that are contrary to habit.' Hippocrates

In a number of wellbeing models, mental and physical health are separated and there is an ongoing concern that mental health is stigmatised: people are more likely to go to their GP than to consult a counsellor. However, there is an undeniable connection between physical and mental health; often mental ill health is manifested as physical symptoms, and at the same time 'a state of ill health can both act as a significant source of stress and also sensitize the person to other sources of stress by reducing their ability to cope' (Cox, 1995).

Before we go into any more detail, it is important to define both physical and mental health and consider societal views and expectations. While the definition of physical health is more straightforward and refers to the wellbeing of our body and its functioning, the definitions of mental health vary. I would like to begin by sharing with you a little about the history of mental health, as it can be very useful when explaining to staff and pupils the stigmas that continue to be associated with mental health in many contexts.

Historical attitudes towards mental health

In their book *Mental Health Concepts*, Claire Waughfield and Teresa Burckhalter (2002) look at how attitudes towards mental health have changed throughout the years. The authors state that although in the past some societies associated mental health with behaviour, some with the heart and some with the mind, 'the Ancient Greeks, Romans and Arabs viewed mental deviations as natural phenomena and treated persons with mental illness humanely'. During the Middle Ages, however, 'the humanitarian ideas concerning persons with mental health were forgotten. The work reverted to superstition, mysticism, witchcraft, and magic. Little was done to treat mental illness.' (Waughfield and Burckhalter, 2002) Similar ideas prevailed during the Renaissance period. George Mora (2008) claims that 'In the Renaissance some of the mentally ill continued to remain at home or in some sort of partial confinement within the extended family. Others may have lived a marginal existence in their own town or may have wandered from place to place as a result of their inner drive or rejection by society. A few considered dangerous to themselves and to others may have ended in jail or some similar confined setting.' People with mental illness may even have been placed in an asylum 'where nonprofessional people were paid to care for them. Mental illness was considered irreversible.'

At the same time, Mora points out that 'many modern psychological and psychopathological concepts originate in the Renaissance […] The word "psychology" is itself a Renaissance product.' It was first used as the title of a book that was published in 1590: Rudolph Goclenius's collection of essays on the origin of the soul, *Psychologia*. One of the characteristic Renaissance figures, Paracelsus, devoted one of his first books, *The Diseases Which Deprive Man of His Reason* (1526), to mental illness. It can be interesting to read his definition, as it shows how understanding of mental illness was beginning to move away from superstition:

> *'In nature there are not only diseases which afflict our body and our health, but many others which deprive us of sound reason, and these are the most serious. While speaking about the natural diseases and observing to what extent and how seriously they afflict various parts of our body, we must not forget to explain the origin of the diseases which deprive man of reason, as we know from experience that they develop out of man's disposition. The present-day clergy of Europe attribute such diseases to ghostly beings and three-fold spirits; we are not inclined to believe them. For nature proves that such statements by earthly Gods are quite incorrect and […] nature is the sole origin of diseases.'*

Yet, the emphasis on witchcraft and a lack of interest in mental health, including a lack of direct observations of patients, both remained among many Renaissance physicians. They also had a tendency to present most psychiatric conditions under the rubric of 'melancholia'. This was accepted as the overwhelming human psychological trait by the medicine of the time. 'Melancholia' attracted the attention of many famous Renaissance figures who researched the phenomena in more detail, including Giovanni da Monte (or Joannes Montanus), Girolamo Fracastoro and Girolamo

Capicacci. They focused on the emotional state of those who experienced melancholia and focused on the early signs of the condition, including sleep disturbances, bad dreams and a tendency toward apathy – which may precede the occurrence of melancholia.

It must also be stressed that explanations of mental disorders 'in terms of "possession" have taken various forms over the course of history'. Those with symptoms of mental ill health were considered to be 'possessed by bad spirits (a practice known as "demonology") and the only way to exercise these bad spirits was with elaborate ritualized ceremonies that frequently involved direct physical attacks on the sufferer's body in an attempt to force out the demons (e.g. through torture, flogging, or starvation)'. (Davey, 2018) Desrosiers and Fleurose (cited in Davey, 2018) claim that 'demonic possession is still a common explanation of psychopathology in some […] areas of the world – especially where witchcraft and voodoo are still important features of the local culture.'

The first mental hospital in England and the second one in Europe, after the Hospital of the Innocents founded in Valencia in 1410, was opened in England in the seventeenth century and was called The Bethlehem Royal Hospital. Waughfield and Burckhalter (2002) describe it: 'Patients were treated as animals and were kept chained in cages. For a small fee, the public was allowed to wander through the hospital and view patients.'

Current attitudes towards mental health

Unfortunately, the stigmas that have been attached to mental health throughout history do still exist in many contexts. People with mental health problems have consistently been treated differently, excluded and even brutalised, and in his book *Psychology*, Davey (2018) claims that this may be caused by 'the misguided views that people with mental health problems may be more violent or unpredictable than people without such problems, or somehow just "different", but none of these beliefs has any basis'. These same misguided views perpetuate today. In a study of over 1,700 adults in the United Kingdom conducted by Crisp et al. (2000), it was found that:

1. 'The most commonly held belief was that people with mental health problems are dangerous – especially those with schizophrenia, alcoholism, or drug dependence.'

2. 'People believed that some mental health problems, such as eating disorders and substance abuse, are self-inflicted.'

3. 'Respondents believed that people with mental health problems are generally hard to talk to.'

Perhaps even more surprisingly, the study found no correlation between these negative beliefs and the respondents' age, existing knowledge of mental health problems and any contact they may have had with people who had a mental health problem. People tended to hold these negative beliefs regardless of all of those factors.' (Davey, 2018)

Defining mental health

Talking about mental health, Dawn Freshwater (2006), author of *Mental Health and Illness*, states that although psychological distress is necessary for human beings to function as it brings awareness and sensitivity, 'there is a point at which psychological distress can topple over into what might be termed or diagnosed as a mental disorder'. However, identifying the point at which 'seemingly "normal" responses can be defined and classified as mental illness is, as one might expect, debatable and highly contentious'.

At this point it must be mentioned that the first extensive system for classifying mental disorders was developed by the World Health Organization, when they added psychological disorders to the International List of Causes of Death (ICD) in 1939. In 1952, the American Psychiatric Association published its first Diagnostic and Statistical Manual (DSM), and the fifth edition of this, DSM-5, is still in use today. However, before proposing a classification system for mental disorders, it was important for the DSM to define a mental health problem. They emphasise distress and disability as the central defining characteristics of a mental health condition. As Davey

(2018) explains, 'Distress relates to the chronic experience of pain or distressing emotions, and disability refers to the fact that the distress can lead to impairment in one or more important areas of functioning, such as education, employment, and dealing with family and social responsibility.'

The following disorders are identified and included in the DSM-5: neurodevelopmental disorders; bipolar and related disorders; anxiety disorders; trauma and stressor-related disorders; dissociative disorders; somatic symptom and related disorders; feeding and eating disorders; sleep–wake disorders; disruptive, impulse-control and conduct disorders; depressive disorders; substance-related and addictive disorders; neurocognitive disorders; schizophrenia; obsessive-compulsive and related disorders; personality disorders.

Although the DSM-5 is criticised for not presenting a complete definition of mental disorders and for the lack of tests of biological functioning, one might argue that it still presents a solid structure for categorising mental illnesses.

However, mental illness is not the same as mental health and defining the latter term is much trickier. There are many definitions of mental health that are overly simplistic, incomplete or subjective. As Freshwater (2006) argues, it is not possible to identify and commit to one specific definition because this 'not only reinforces the belief that the concept of mental health can be pinpointed and concretised, but of course it is in itself also too simplistic and partial'. Mental health is a 'continuum' rather than a 'polarised dichotomy, with people positioned at various points depending on life events (external factors), genetic inheritance and stages of development (internal factors)'.

How can we use this complex knowledge to enhance our pastoral care practices? Here are some takeaways:

Physical health: Sleep, screen time and healthy eating can be covered within our pastoral curriculum. We should remain sensitive to the physical needs of all pupils (and they will vary significantly) to create a truly inclusive pastoral community.

Mental health: What can we do to work towards creating a stigma-free environment? Creating strong foundations and educating staff and pupils are both key and can be achieved through the pastoral curriculum and INSET sessions, as well as ensuring that school life is rooted in values and a strong ethos reflected in our policies.

2. Family and social relations

'Human beings are social animals; we devote a significant portion of our brain just to dealing with interactions with other humans.'
Jamais Cascio

Talking about wellbeing, Keyes (1998) states that 'although the existing models emphasize private features of well-being, individuals remain embedded in social structures and communities, and face countless social tasks and challenges'. This means that family and social relationships are a crucial element when considering a person's overall wellbeing. The researcher proposes the following definition of social wellbeing: '[S]ocial well-being is the appraisal of one's circumstances and functioning in society.' Keyes identifies five social wellbeing dimensions:

- **Social integration:** the sense that you belong to a community.
- **Social acceptance:** having positive feelings towards others and being brought into social interactions by others.
- **Social contribution:** feeling like you can contribute.
- **Social actualisation:** being confident about the opportunities society provides and being able to fulfil the need for personal growth.
- **Social coherence:** understanding and caring about the world around you, being able to sustain harmonious relationships with one another and contribute to positive social growth and stability.

These are important elements that contribute to creating and nurturing social wellbeing in a school environment. Schools play a critical role in developing social and emotional skills that are crucial to social wellbeing. As Barry et al. (2017) say, 'A broad range of skills, including cognitive, social and emotional skills, are needed by young people to develop positively and be successful in life.' Ensuring that these skills are developed as part of the curriculum is an essential element of effective and proactive pastoral care. Those in charge of pastoral care should ensure the school takes a more holistic approach to the development of their pupils, and embedding many of the elements discussed in this book – character education, PSHE and RSE – is crucial to supporting the five social wellbeing dimensions mentioned by Keyes (1998).

Ensuring social wellbeing at school is not just about developing a more holistic curriculum, however. Proactive pastoral care should also focus on creating a school culture and community that ensures all pupils can integrate and feel as though they belong. Keyes (1998) states that 'healthy individuals feel that they are a part of society. Integration is therefore the extent to which people feel they have something in common with others who constitute their social reality.' So, what can schools do to ensure that pupils feel that they belong, that they are a part of the 'school society'?

Eliminating bullying

Dealing with instances of bullying, which has a detrimental effect on pupils' social wellbeing, has always been a key part of pastoral care, although often it is more reactive than proactive. A head of year is informed of a specific incident and they deal with the issue as it arises, escalating it through the pastoral care system if required. However, proactive pastoral care should focus on what schools can do to eliminate bullying before such incidents become critical. So what can schools do about this? And would we need different approaches for boys and girls?

Tim Fields, co-author of *Bullycide in America* (edited by High, 2012), claims that bullying *is* different among boys and girls. He says, 'quite simply, girls have a superior social intelligence... Both genders bully, but girls are better at it; they are more switched on to the nuances of social interaction and use psychological forms that are harder to detect and easier to deny'. In her book *Queen Bees and Wannabes*, Rosalind Wiseman (2002) warns that the effects of bullying on victims can be devastating and long term: 'Girls' relationships with each other are really the key to their survival, but they can also be the key to their destruction.' These statements are echoed by Rachel Simmons (2011), who suggests that 'unlike boys, who tend to bully acquaintances or strangers, girls frequently attack within tightly knit friendship networks, making aggression harder to identify and intensifying the damage to the victims.' Simmons claims that girls use body language and relationships to bully, instead of fists and knives.

How can we, as pastoral leaders, be proactive in dealing with bullying? As you know, culture is the starting point. We must aim to create a culture of diversity, inclusivity and kindness. We should also enable young people to gain a higher degree of self-awareness and assertiveness as well as educating them about managing conflict and controlling emotions. If an incident has occurred, aftercare is vital: provide opportunities for restorative work and care that could prevent incidents from recurring.

Building effective community partnerships

'Effective partnerships across the education, youth, family and community sectors are critical to sustaining evidence-based programmes that can bring about enduring change to the lives of young people.' (National Academies of Sciences, Engineering and Medicine, 2017) So, how can we ensure that we design an effective community intervention that will support a school culture in which all pupils feel a sense of belonging? The views of the community must be sought and incorporated, hence the involvement of teachers, pupils and their parents is recommended from the very beginning. According to the Harvard University Center on Child Development, 'the single most common factor for children who develop resilience is at least one stable and committed relationship with a supportive parent, caregiver, or other adult. These relationships provide the personalized responsiveness, scaffolding, and protection that buffer children from developmental disruption. They also build key capacities – such as the ability to plan, monitor, and regulate behavior – that enable children to respond adaptively to adversity and thrive.'

It is also important to acknowledge that although schools can contribute positively to creating and nurturing a culture favourable for social wellbeing, they only have limited capability to influence family relationships, which are crucial to young people's social wellbeing. The Foresight Mental Capital and Wellbeing Project (2018) research project summary states that 'new evidence confirms that early child–parent and child–carer relationships are particularly important to later flourishing, both socially and cognitively.' There are a number of factors that impact on these relationships, including the parent's level of knowledge around effective parenting and child development. The same project found that the care that children receive in the Early Years also impacts on a young person's social development, and this is another area where a secondary school can have no immediate influence. Nonetheless, there are proactive steps that can be taken to bring about long-term change in both of these aspects. This includes working in close partnership with feeder schools to ensure that the development of social wellbeing begins at the earliest possible age. Engaging parents in pastoral matters and their child's wellbeing is another critical step that I will look at in more detail in Chapter 5.

3. Emotions and mood

'Anyone can become angry – that is easy. But to be angry with the right person, to the right degree, at the right time, for the right purpose, and in the right way – this is not easy.' Aristotle

What is emotional wellbeing? According to Schutte et al. (2002), emotional wellbeing 'includes positive mood and high self-esteem'. Emotions and mood are very much interlinked, but often 'distinctions between them are clouded, in part, because an emotion and a mood may feel very much the same from the perspective of an individual experiencing either' (Beedie et al., 2005). At the same time, they represent two different phenomena. Mood has been often referred to as an affective state of mind or feelings without particular triggers. Research indicates that mood is also a lasting characteristic, similar to a personality trait (Watson et al., 1988). When drawing a distinction between emotions and mood, Barry (2018) states, 'Emotions relate to how we feel, lasting for relatively short durations, usually minutes to hours. If lasting for longer periods – hours or perhaps days – we call them moods.'

Like mental health, 'emotional health isn't an all-or-nothing proposition. It exists along a continuum.' As Maureen Healy (2018) says in her book *The Emotionally Healthy Child*, emotional health is a spectrum ranging from negative to positive. The signs of negative emotional health include harbouring negativity, quick reactions and careless choices that may injure ourselves or others. Positive emotional health is exhibited by healthy habits, emotional intelligence, careful choices and awareness of the self and others. It's important to note that having positive emotional health doesn't mean you will feel good all the time. As Healy explains, 'it's about being an authentic person who feels his or her feelings, learns to constructively express them (not to hold onto them), and form healthy relationships, despite whatever challenges appear in the outer world.'

There exist many definitions of emotions, but there is still no clear and agreed definition despite extensive studies and research in this area. In the 1980s, Fehr and Russell (1984) wrote that 'Everyone knows what an emotion is, until asked to give a definition. Then, it seems, no one knows.' Damasio (1999) believed 'that emotion feeling is a consequence of the neurobiological (body) expression.' The researchers Kleinginna and Kleinginna (1981) explored a vast total of 92 definitions around the concept of emotion. Their research shows that, even 40 years ago, there was no consensus on how to define emotion and whether it was useful in the scientific framework (Caruana, 2011). There are, however, some useful common themes we can draw out of the research.

Defining and categorising emotions

Firstly, some researchers examine the link between emotion, behaviour and a physical response. For example, in their book *Discovering Psychology*, Don and Sandra Hockenbury (2007) define emotion as 'a complex psychological state that involves three distinct components: a subjective experience, a physiological response, and a behavioral or expressive response'. Similarly, in his book *Emotional Resilience*, Dr Harry Barry (2018) states that 'Emotions are created by thoughts. They are also associated with specific behavioural patterns. Some emotions are also associated with physical symptoms.'

There have also been attempts in the literature to identify lists of basic human emotions. According to Sara Dellantonio and Luigi Pastore (2017), although 'humans certainly have emotions that are much more complex than those exhibited by animals… some of their emotions seem to be more basic and these might also be shared by animals and indeed have a biological basis.' During the 1970s, Izard identified ten basic emotions, while Ekman put forward a list of six basic emotions that he suggested were universally experienced in all human cultures:

Izard's list of basic emotions	Ekman's list of basic emotions
• Interest	• Happiness
• Joy	• Sadness
• Surprise	• Disgust
• Anger	• Fear
• Contempt	• Surprise
• Disgust	• Anger
• Distress	
• Fear	
• Guilt	
• Shame	

Ekman later expanded his list of basic emotions to include such things as pride, shame, embarrassment and excitement.

In his interview with Sieff (2015), Schore discusses how human emotions develop from relatively basic to much more complex as we grow up. Schore claims that 'when we are born our emotions are relatively crude – we are happy or we are upset. As we develop, our emotions become increasingly differentiated, shaded and refined, yet also integrated. We learn to create blends of different emotions simultaneously. Things are no longer wholly good, or wholly bad. We can feel anger and compassion with somebody simultaneously.' Similarly, Feldman Barrett (2017) uses an interesting analogy to explain how emotions can be categorised, likening them to cookies: 'There are crisp ones, chewy ones, sweet ones, savory ones, large, small, flat, rounded, rolled, sandwiched, floured, flourless, and more. The members of the category "Cookie" vary tremendously but are deemed equivalent for some purpose: to be a tasty snack or dessert [...] Even within a more fine-grained category like "Chocolate Chip Cookie", there is still diversity created by the type of chocolate, the amount of flour, the ratio of brown sugar to white sugar, the fat content of the butter, and the time spent chilling the dough. Likewise, any category of emotion such as "Happiness" or "Guilt" is filled with variety.'

More simply, Harry Barry (2018) distinguishes between four types of emotions:

- **Positive:** joy, happiness, pleasure, love, awe, trust, contentment, peacefulness.
- **Negative:** anger, fear, guilt, shame, hurt, jealousy, emotional pain, sadness, loss.
- **Healthy negative:** grief, loss, sadness, disappointment, annoyance, irritation, regret, remorse.
- **Unhealthy negative:** anxiety, depression, anger, rage, emotional pain, shame, guilt, jealousy, envy, hurt.

When questioning what emotion is, Naar and Teroni (2018) summarise that 'it is a psychological entry of some sort', adding that 'rich and lively philosophical debates have failed to generate any stable picture regarding the nature of emotions that extends much beyond this platitude.' Despite this, Naar and Teroni do succeed in identifying certain features that the majority of philosophers would agree are exemplified by emotions:

- Emotions are felt.

- Emotions are intentional phenomena and directed towards a particular thing in the world around us, for example, we might be amused by a joke, sad at the death of a friend or proud of being a self-made man or woman.

- Emotions are closely connected with our own evaluation of these things, for example, we positively evaluate the joke or negatively evaluate the friend's death.

- Emotions are relatively short-lived: they usually endure for no longer than a few hours. This is in contrast to other related phenomena, such as character traits or sentiments, which may last for a substantial portion of a person's lifetime.

The relationship between emotions and social relationships

Some researchers focus on the links between emotions and social relationships. For example, Schore claims that 'emotional expressions are crucial to the development and regulation of interpersonal relationships'. However, we need to bear in mind that not all emotions are expressed and in some cases people can deliberately or habitually feign the expression of an emotion without actually experiencing the emotion, using facial or verbal cues. This could be to mislead or to 'refer to an emotion that is not currently experienced'. Feldman Barrett (2017) also claims that 'some facial movements have meaning, but others do not, and right now, we know precious little about how people figure out which is which, other than that context is somehow crucial (body language, social situation, cultural expectation, etc.)'. In other words, how an emotion is expressed by one person may be completely different to how another person expresses that very same emotion. If someone raises an eyebrow, for example, the meaning of this isn't necessarily the same each time, and we don't even know whether this message is always emotional. As Feldman Barrett says, 'We cannot claim, with any reasonable certainty, that each emotion has a diagnostic facial expression.' This needs to be taken into account when dealing with young people. As pastoral leaders, we are taught to notice, to look for verbal and non-verbal signs, but we should never expect or assume anything: just because a pupil is not explicitly displaying expected non-verbal signs of emotions, it doesn't mean that the problem is not there.

When looking at how emotions are made, Feldman Barrett (2017), who has done extensive research in this area, distinguishes between the 'classical view of emotions' and 'the theory of constructed emotion', as they 'tell vastly different stories of how we experience the world':

- **The classical view of emotions:** Events in the world around us cause emotional reactions inside of us. This is how most of us would traditionally understand our emotions.

- **The theory of constructed emotion:** Our brain invisibly constructs everything we experience, including emotions. This doesn't necessarily match what is happening in our daily lives and involves simulation, concepts and degeneracy.

The researcher argues that the classical view of emotions is based on misconceptions and certain inaccuracies; her own experiments revealed that everyone tested expressed their emotions using the same words, such as 'angry', 'sad' and 'afraid', but they didn't always mean the same thing. One particular example is that people often didn't distinguish between feelings of anxiety and feelings of depression.

At the same time, Feldman Barrett explains the 'theory of constructed emotion' in the following way: 'In every waking moment, your brain uses past experience, organized as concepts, to guide your actions and give your sensations meaning. When the concepts involved are emotion concepts, your brain constructs instances of emotion.' According to this theory, simulation is 'the default mode for all mental activity. It also holds a key to unlocking the mystery of how the brain creates emotions.' Our brains guess what is happening around us, and then translate the information from our sensory organs (such as our eyes, ears and nose) into a theory, to give this information meaning. Our brain selects what it believes to be relevant and then ignores everything else. Feldman Barrett points to scientific evidence that 'shows that what we see, hear, touch, taste, and smell are largely simulations of the world, not reactions to it'. Some thinkers even speculate that this is how we understand language, how we feel empathy and how we remember, imagine and dream. Feldman Barrett concludes that variation exists in how we experience and express emotions and this is something we must appreciate if we are to understand emotions more fully. This theory gives us a lot to think about in terms of our social relationships and wellbeing, as it puts the uniqueness of each individual at the forefront and emphasises the need for greater understanding, empathy and compassion.

Emotional trauma

When researching emotions, a great focus has been placed on nurturing and emotional trauma, particularly in childhood. According to Kalsched (quoted in Sieff, 2015), how humans develop 'as an integrated whole' depends on the social and emotional environment in which they grow up. This environment impacts on a person's creativity, confidence and sense of self, and how well they learn to protect their emotional self in a healthy way. If a person's sense of self is 'repeatedly threatened', for example if they are 'made to feel inadequate', this healthy development will be compromised. Of course, emotional trauma can have an impact on us whenever it occurs throughout our lives, but as Sieff adds, 'the consequences of suffering trauma during infancy and childhood are particularly significant and long-lasting'. He explains that this 'is because early relationships with parents and other caregivers (known as "attachment relationships") influence the development of our emotional brains, fear response and reproductive physiology'. If a child's parents abuse or neglect them – or are simply unable to understand and respond to their needs (perhaps due to their own emotional difficulties or mental ill health) – this child 'will develop along different biological pathways'.

Neglect or a lack of sufficient care in early childhood can also impact the ability of the brain to regulate emotions in a healthy way. As Sieff (2015) states, 'Good enough early nurturing fosters the neural networks (located in the right hemisphere of the brain) which enables us to regulate our emotions healthily.' This not only allows us to trust our emotions and respond to the social networks around us, but it also builds a sense of inner security. If this early nurturing is lacking, the development of the right hemisphere is compromised. We struggle to respond to those around us and cannot regulate our emotions successfully. We find ourselves overloaded with unregulated emotions and we struggle to cope with this level of emotional overload, meaning 'we unconsciously learn to dissociate from our emotions'. Regular dissociation can lead to emotional instability and insecurity.

How can we support children who have experienced emotional trauma? We must always go back to the culture of the school, its pastoral structure and staff development. A 2017 green paper (Department of Health and Department for Education, 2017) states, 'There is evidence that appropriately-trained and supported [school] staff can achieve results comparable to those achieved by trained therapists in delivering a number of interventions addressing mild to moderate mental health problems'. This could lead us back to the debate of how much staff should be involved in mental health interventions. Irrespective of differences in opinions, it is important that all staff have pastoral training to increase awareness, confidence and understanding of issues faced in our communities.

Helping students to talk about emotional health

So, from all of these incredibly varied definitions, what should we focus on when we introduce and discuss such a complex topic with young people in schools? Firstly, we need to emphasise that emotional health isn't about denying negative feelings but about learning to cope with them and face up to them with courage and bravery – and this is a lifelong journey. Emotional health is about making better choices, even when you are experiencing a challenging emotion such as anger, jealousy, loss, betrayal or disappointment. This can be difficult for adults but even more so for children, who, as Maureen Healy (2018) says, 'tend to have feelings that are bigger, faster, and more intense, which means they need to gather even more courage to help them handle these epic emotions'.

After three decades of research and practical experience, Brackett and his colleagues (2019) have identified the following skills to become 'emotion scientists'. These are the skills that I would recommend focusing on building with young people to enable them to improve their emotional health and balance:

- recognising our own emotions and those of others
- understanding those feelings and determining their source
- labelling emotions with a nuanced vocabulary
- expressing our feelings in accordance with cultural norms and social contexts in a way that tries to inform and that invites empathy from the listener
- regulating emotions, rather than letting them regulate us, by finding practical strategies for dealing with what we and others feel.

As adults responsible for our young people, we should attempt to empower our pupils to have strategies for recognising and expressing emotions by providing relevant knowledge, opportunities for reflection and, most importantly, by creating a culture of belonging and acceptance.

4. Spiritual and moral goodness

'A man may be the greatest philosopher in the world but a child in religion. When a man has developed a high state of spirituality he

can understand that the kingdom of heaven is within him.' Swami Vivekananda

As we have seen, spiritual and moral goodness have been mentioned by many philosophers over the centuries. However, as Glenn Cupit (2007) notes, 'spirituality is generally ignored in human development texts and never treated as an essential component of development.' It is no surprise that spirituality has not featured on the pastoral curriculum in schools. It is a tricky area to approach and there is unease among staff trying to tackle various sensitive topics while taking into account young people's ethnic, cultural and religious backgrounds. I have included both the words 'spiritual' and 'moral' to ensure that anyone, irrespective of their religious beliefs, can relate to this area of wellbeing. In order to avoid any misinterpretations, I am going to define it as an area of wellbeing that is concerned with personal growth and human spirit.

According to Daniel Scott (2009), 'One's understanding of spirituality is rooted in one's cultural, religious/non-religious, social and personal locations, traditions, and experiences.' I would therefore like to take a couple of paragraphs to consider spirituality from the perspective of two major religions: Christianity and Islam.

If we turn to Christianity, we can see three basic elements identified in the Bible: spirit, soul and body (Thessalonians 5:23). According to the author Witness Lee (1994), 'we have two main organs. One is the body as our outward organ, which is full of functions. But we also have an intrinsic organ within us – our spirit…'. Lee calls for us to study, exercise and care for our spirit, believing that if we do not, we will never 'enjoy God', 'be spiritual' or 'grow in the divine life'.

In Islam, **rūḥ** is a person's immortal, essential self – pneuma, i.e. the 'spirit'. According to the *Oxford Dictionary of Islam*, **rūḥ** is a 'spirit, breath (of life)'. It is used in the Quran 21 times, 'referring to the divine spirit in the sense of communication of life force'. It is 'often interpreted as an immaterial, immortal element of a living being, as well as the true self, or soul, apart from the body [and is] also a designation for

Jesus and the angel Gabriel'. It's 'often used interchangeably with nafs (self), although Sufis distinguish between **rūḥ** as the higher principle of soul and nafs as the "lower" or "animal" self'.

Spirituality has been defined in many different ways depending on whether it has been considered from religious, humanist or psychological perspectives, and as we can see from the examples of Christianity and Islam, even within the religious perspective we can come across a variety of definitions. However, there are some common themes in many of the definitions from a religious perspective. As James Nelson (2009) writes, 'Religious conceptions of spirituality generally involve **thick** definitions that are rich in allusions to specific beliefs and practices, as opposed to **thin** or generic "one size fits all" definitions that focus more on natural experiences, personal values, or connectedness.' For example, the Centre of Spiritual Development in Childhood and Adolescence, which has strong religious roots, defines spirituality as 'the process of growing the intrinsic human capacity for self-transcendence, in which the self is embedded in something greater than the self, including the sacred. It is the developmental "engine" that propels the search for connectedness, meaning, purpose and contribution. It is shaped both within and outside of religious traditions, beliefs, and practices.' (Benson et al., 2003) At the same time, Jernigan's (2001) definition of Christian spirituality is very different: 'the organization (centering) of individual and collective life around loving relationships with God, neighbor, self, and all of creation – responding to the love of God revealed in Jesus Christ and at work through the Holy Spirit'.

A number of researchers have separated the notions of religion and spirituality. Rayburn (2004) claims that 'separating the two has the advantage of recognizing that a kind of broadly defined spirituality is quite possible for those outside of religious traditions and communities.' At the same time, I agree with Zinnbauer and his colleagues (1999, quoted in Nelson, 2009), who have pointed out that 'researchers who draw a strict distinction between religion and spirituality often polarise the concepts in value-laden ways, with organised, communal religion defined in negative terms and individualistic spirituality in positive terms. In their view, these types of definitions can tell us more about the values or prejudices of the investigators than the phenomenon they are studying'.

For me, being spiritual is not a separate nature or characteristic that we have but an inseparable part of who we are and what we do. Personal growth and spirituality are about embarking on the journey of self-discovery and inner growth, focusing on deeper layers of self and following dreams and aspirations.

Spirituality and moral goodness are not just linked to our own personal growth but also linked to our social behaviour. Individual subjective wellbeing is both an outcome of social systems and a factor in their functioning. This dual role leads me to describe the relationship between individual flourishing, the product of authentic wellbeing and environment as a two-way relationship. Under certain circumstances, it would be possible to assume that a certain environment might stop or slow down individual flourishing, but on the other hand, an individual who is flourishing is likely to influence the environment in a positive way. This means that if we are able to create a culture of wellbeing in our schools, the improved wellbeing of individual pupils, which is an outcome of this, may in turn lead to an even more positive atmosphere where everyone can flourish. Creating this positive wellbeing cycle is the cornerstone of proactive pastoral care.

*

Having thought of this four-part wellbeing model, I didn't just consider the various factors involved; I thought about the wellbeing philosophy behind them. I was particularly eager to have a model that could be used by teachers and pupils and applied to the real and the digital world. Having analysed various wellbeing theories, established and current, I have created a hybrid model that incorporates features present across various theories. I would also like to use the term 'authentic' to define wellbeing in order to highlight its subjective nature – in other words, wellbeing must be true for the individual in question.

If implemented collaboratively with care and sensitivity, this model would help us to truly embed wellbeing in our school culture and enhance proactive pastoral structures as it could:

- Provide a structured approach to wellbeing by focusing on four distinct areas.
- Bring different areas of school closer together: academic, pastoral and co-curricular are all closely interlinked and contribute to creating and nourishing the overall wellbeing of the community.
- Create pastoral structures with scope to act proactively.
- Identify potential gaps in our provision and areas to focus on.
- Communicate our wellbeing mission to the wider community with more clarity and conviction.

Introducing the model to children

The four wellbeing areas that we have looked at in this chapter can be presented in the following way:

Figure 3.1 *The wellbeing garden*

We can see a garden with four trees and some tools in the middle. Each tree represents a particular area of wellbeing:

Tree 1: Family and social relations
Tree 2: Spiritual and moral goodness
Tree 3: Emotions and mood
Tree 4: Physical and mental health

The tools in the middle are the resources we need to look after our wellbeing. Each tree might require a different tool, just like we might need different resources to nurture different areas of our wellbeing. The four areas of wellbeing can be introduced to pupils using this model.

There is a lot we can do in the classroom using this wellbeing model, depending on pupils' age and previous knowledge. Here are some of the activities you could consider or you could instead use them as a basis to develop your own wellbeing activities:

1. Pupils can design their own wellbeing garden. They can use their favourite plants or flowers, which will give them ownership.

2. They can look at what tools they would need to ensure that their plants and flowers flourish.

3. As a class, you can discuss how despite the fact that one plant or flower might not be well, the others can still keep on flourishing. This will show pupils that although they might not be happy with certain areas of their lives, they can still find fulfilment in others. This exercise will also allow pupils to see what areas of wellbeing need more of their attention.

4. You can think of external situations, for example, what happens when it starts raining? This is a great opportunity to talk about healthy negative emotions. Rain can represent something positive; rain is part of the water cycle, just like grief and loss, for example, are inevitable parts of our lives.

Reflections

1. How can you incorporate the wellbeing garden model into your teaching?

_____

_____

_____

2. How could it contribute to our wellbeing culture?

_____

_____

_____

3. What are you doing already that contributes to the following areas of wellbeing:

Physical and mental health	Emotional health	Social health	Spiritual health

4. What other opportunities could we offer to enhance these wellbeing areas?

_____

_____

_____

4 Character education

Overview

This chapter will:

- discuss what character education is and what it is not
- link character education with proactive pastoral care
- consider opportunities to embed character education across the curriculum.

Character education is an important element of proactive pastoral care. It has been more apt than ever before during the COVID-19 pandemic: our young people need resilience to deal with the uncertainties and challenges of the current situation successfully, and in a manner that enables them to remain mentally, physically, emotionally and socially healthy. Pupils need to have a well-developed moral compass and personal skills.

Character education and development have been gaining increasing attention within the education sector in the UK. Research conducted by the Jubilee Centre for Character and Virtues at the University of Birmingham – 'Character Education in UK Schools' (Arthur et al., 2015) – showed that 'a concern for the development of a child's whole character is central to good education and practice'. The good news is that the majority of teachers involved in the research felt their school already had a 'whole-school approach to character building'. However, the research pointed to 'weak links in the education system, which suggest that moral education needs to be prioritised within a greater number of schools'. To raise the profile of character education, the Department for Education launched character education grants – a scheme 'to fund schools and organisations promoting traits such as resilience and respect'. The grants were available to schools 'that use activities such as sports, debating or music to provide a rounded learning experience for children'. But character education is much more than those activities, and to me it feels wrong to have a tick box of things schools need to do to show that they take character education seriously.

What is character education?

So, if character education isn't a tick box of extra-curricular activities, what is it? Before answering this question, it is important to look first at what character education is not. According to the researchers Nucci and Narvaez (2014), 'Character education is not the same as behaviour control, discipline, training, or indoctrination, it is much broader. Character is an inclusive term for the individual as a whole.' Character education reinforces the 'whole child' agenda that shifts the emphasis from academic achievement to long-term learning and development. It is therefore important to remember that:

- Character education is **not** about 'fixing' our young people.
- It is **not** about giving them pre-determined strategies on how to get along with their peers, teachers or family members.
- It is **not** about reinforcing accepted rules and teaching pupils right from wrong with the aim of improving their behaviour.

Establishing sanctions and rewards systems can lead to temporary changes in behaviour, but the outcomes will not be sustainable. Character education requires us to dig deeper and look at the moral principles, ethos and virtues that underpin human behaviours. It is defined by Dr Thomas Lickona (1996) as: 'The deliberate effort by schools, families and communities to help young people understand, care about, and act upon core ethical values.' Although we couldn't be thoroughly prepared for something like the COVID-19 pandemic, having a strong moral compass would have helped young people and adults to navigate through challenging situations and show compassion and empathy to others.

What is important to note is that it is difficult to measure the effectiveness of character education as its outcomes are 'a complex set of psychological characteristics that motivate one to function as a moral agent' (Berkowitz, 1997). This is a big turn-off for schools where culture is data-driven rather than people-driven. Another challenge is that we have different concepts and understandings of moral values. This will cause problems for some, as we are used to operating in evidence-, results- and accountability-driven environments. We are often forced to use quick-fix solutions that will bring immediate results without dealing with the root of the problem or problems. Berkowitz (1997) echoes this: 'Effective character education is not adding a program or set of programs to a school. Rather it is a transformation of the culture and life of the school.' He goes on, 'Effective character education tends to include: professional development; student interactive pedagogical strategies; an explicit focus on character/ethics; direct training of social and emotional competencies; modelling of character; aligned classroom/behaviour management strategies and community service and/or service learning.' (Berkowitz and Bier, 2007) Let's have a look at some of the areas that will fall under proactive pastoral care.

Character education and proactive pastoral care

Pastoral care is everyone's responsibility; when we are dealing with a change in school culture, we are dealing with many different components that form educational communities: beliefs, values, climate, relationships, patterns of behaviour, written or unwritten rules and, most importantly, 'the way we do things'. It is vital to ensure that staff are given training to develop their own personal skills and time to gain a deeper understanding of the issues and processes relating to wellbeing and proactive pastoral care. This can be achieved through various sustainable forms of CPD activities that enable teacher growth and teacher change through reflection and collaboration. Examples might include coaching, action research projects, staff book clubs, Lesson Study or staff working groups.

Character education across the curriculum

In terms of curriculum, many would consider PSHE lessons to be the only platform from which to promote character education. However, we can do so through other subjects in a less formal way. Thus, we can promote resilience and grit in PE lessons, empathy in religious education, and diversity and understanding in languages education. Most subjects, well taught, will enable the learner to think, to feel and to see differently. If they do not do this, they are not worth teaching. But some experiences transform the very essence of the person. These transformative experiences always involve a deep personal enlightenment on the part of the young person – a greater understanding of who they are and how they fit into the world. They can happen as an active participant or as a passive observer. They could happen on or in front of a stage, in or in front of an orchestra or band, or in front of an easel or at a gallery. Participation in and appreciation of drama, music and art are among the most powerfully transformative experiences our young people can have because they require you to express yourself. To do so requires you to examine and understand yourself and others, which brings us back to self-awareness, something that is crucial for our wellbeing.

It is essential that, as teachers, we consistently work together at promoting character education. We should strive to demonstrate by example what is healthy; at the same time, we are human and it is natural that from time to time we would demonstrate something that is not particularly healthy. The main thing to do when this happens is to show self-awareness. Many teachers I have worked with said to me that they feel bad when their lives don't match their self-imposed wellbeing expectations. I would always reply that it is not ethical to set unrealistic standards for our pupils, and it's a great opportunity to distinguish between ongoing and long-term wellbeing. I define ongoing wellbeing as daily wellbeing that can go up and down depending on the triggers. Our long-term wellbeing will depend on the tools or resources we have to overcome bad days and to appreciate good ones.

It is also my experience that many teachers would pigeon-hole themselves as academic leaders; my belief is that if we work with young people, we are all pastoral leaders by default. For example, through ensuring academic rigour, we can all promote discipline, academic honesty and hard work. These are important qualities and skills that our young people need to succeed not only at school, but in life. It is our responsibility to provide opportunities for students to develop good character. The Jubilee Centre (Birdwell et al., 2015) identifies four main categories of good character:

- moral virtues, such as courage, honesty, humility, empathy and gratitude
- intellectual values, such as curiosity and critical thinking
- performance virtuals, such as resilience, application and self-regulation
- civic virtues, such as acts of service and volunteering.

What activities could schools offer that would allow pupils to put these values into action?

- Co-curricular and enrichment activities that build collaborative skills, communication skills, creativity and critical thinking (the 4 Cs). Depending on the context, the following activities could be integrated in the co-curricular provision:
  - STEM: science, technology, engineering and maths clubs (you could try out subjects such as architecture, robotics, computing or gaming or virtual reality)
  - subject podcasts
  - art clubs
  - drama productions

- dance clubs
- music and singing clubs
- chess clubs
- LEGO™ clubs
- debating clubs
- book clubs
- critical thinking at a critical age (such as decision-making, problem solving, reasoning, evaluating, questioning)
- journalism (what about a student newspaper or magazine?)
- social or environmental activism (thinking about wildlife or recycling)
- faith space
- virtual teams (making decisions under pressure and developing strategic thinking).

- Extra and co-curricular activities that build endurance, stamina and resilience. You could try:
  - sports practices
  - competitions and fixtures
  - fitness
  - running clubs
  - outdoor adventure learning.

- Leadership training and creating responsibility posts for the pupils (including peer support groups with a particular focus), such as:
  - digital leaders
  - mental health and wellbeing ambassadors
  - diversity and inclusion societies
  - buddy support system
  - student council

- ◦ student government
- ◦ student SLT.
- Co-curricular and enrichment activities that promote civic and moral virtues, for example:
  - ◦ community service volunteering opportunities
  - ◦ fundraising
  - ◦ securing links with outside agencies and social entrepreneurship.

All co-curricular, character-building activities contribute to the overall wellbeing of pupils as they meet certain psychological needs. Mangal and Mangal (2008) call them a 'safety valve' that enables pupils to release 'surplus energy', stating: 'Catharsis and sublimation of various emotions and the proper form of outlet or expression through these activities helps in the proper training of emotions. These activities also help in meeting the individual differences of the students in terms of their varying tastes, temperaments, interests, aptitudes, capacities and talents.'

Through research, the Jubilee Centre found that one of the main things that schools with a strong approach to developing character had in common was assigning 'a key person... often a senior member of staff, supported by the head and senior leadership team (SLT), who is responsible for character education throughout the school.' (Birdwell et al., 2015)

However, it must be emphasised that whether a caretaker, or a headteacher, it is vital that every single member of the school community accepts shared responsibility for character education so that it becomes 'part of the fabric of the community' (Gelpi, 2008): an integral, natural part of school life. It is clear that character education underpins proactive pastoral care. It needs to be reflected in the school ethos and values and incorporated into all parts of day-to-day school life and routine. As Gelpi (2008) said, 'Everything in a school's moral life affects character, for good or for ill.'

Reflections

1. How does character education underpin proactive pastoral care in your setting?

_____

_____

_____

2. What opportunities do your curriculum and teaching provide for character development?

_____

_____

_____

3. What opportunities does your co-curricular provision offer?

_____

_____

_____

4. What are you already doing towards building character education in the four areas that underpin wellbeing?

Physical and mental health	Emotional health	Social health	Spiritual health

5. What else could you do to embed character development and education?

_____

_____

_____

6. Who else could you involve to enhance your provision?

_____

_____

_____

5 Community pastoral engagement

Overview

This chapter will:

- compare parental involvement and parental engagement
- explain why parental engagement is important
- discuss parental engagement with pastoral care
- offer a model for parental engagement
- provide a set of practical strategies to secure parental engagement with pastoral care.

Parents, staff, pupils and governors are all responsible for creating and nurturing a culture of safety and security for our young people. The problem is that a number of parents are mainly interested in the academic progress of their child, and pastoral engagement is not necessarily their priority until things go wrong. Parents tend to be responsive rather than proactive in their engagement; at the same time they are and should act as active participants in the safeguarding of their children's wellbeing as it is their duty to do so.

Parental involvement versus parental engagement

Looking at the literature, you might have come across 'parental involvement' and 'parental engagement', but what is the difference between them? Simply put, some would use these terms as synonymous without identifying any particular differences between the two. For me, involvement is only a starting point: parents are responsive or reactive to the school's instructions, they listen to the school, attend parents' evening and do as they are told, while parental engagement means becoming active participants, working together with the school. Active parental engagement is an important part of proactive pastoral care.

The truth is that parental involvement is not clearly or consistently defined in the academic literature. Researchers Harris and Goodall (2007) say it has been described as: 'representing many different parental behaviours; parenting practices such as parental aspirations for their child's academic achievement; parental communication with their children about school; parental participation in school activities; parental communications with teachers about their child; and parental rules at home which are considered to be education-related'. Hornby and Lafaele (2011) explore this further and state that parental participation includes 'home-based parental involvement, such as listening to children read and supervision of homework, as well as school-based parental involvement, such as attending parent education workshops and parent-teacher meetings.'

Although all these activities are valid and useful, it is important that parents take the initiative and become more proactive rather than remain reactive and wait for instructions from the school. Goodall and Montgomery (2014) explain that 'engagement' suggests not just 'activity' but 'some feeling of ownership of that activity which is greater than is present with simple involvement. This means that parental engagement will involve a greater commitment, a greater ownership of action, than will parental involvement with schools.' Family engagement consultant Nicola Morgan (2017) sums this up nicely and affirms that 'parent involvement starts with the school and parent engagement begins with the parent'.

Why is parental engagement important?

Morgan (2017) claims that 'Research has shown that family engagement is one of the strong predictors of students' success.' To support her point, she quotes the research conducted by Professor Charles Desforges and Alberto Abouchaar (2003), which found that:

- 'Parental engagement is strongly positively influenced by the child's level of attainment; the higher the level of attainment, the more parents get involved.

- Parental engagement in the form of "at-home good parenting" has a significant positive effect on children's achievement and adjustment even after all other factors shaping attainment have been taken out of the equation. In the primary age range, the impact caused by different levels of parental involvement is much greater than differences associated with variations in the quality of schools. The scale of impact is evident across all social classes and all ethnic groups.'

In their book *Do Parents Know They Matter: Raising achievement through parental engagement*, researchers Harris et al. (2009) 'synthesize contemporary research evidence about parental engagement and learning'. In brief, the researchers show that parental engagement has significant benefits for students and their achievement.

The benefits of parental engagement in terms of academic attainment are clear. However, we should remain mindful of the risk that this approach carries: 'Parents may place excessive pressure on students to academically excel. This may be detrimental to children's wellbeing, as there is increasing recognition that a lack of social and emotional competence can adversely affect student wellbeing and overall academic achievement.' (Emerson et al., 2012)

Most, if not all, the research connects parental engagement with attainment, therefore focusing on the academic side of things, but what about parental engagement with pastoral care?

Parental engagement with pastoral care

How do we establish much-needed parental engagement with pastoral care? When I ask this question, many colleagues talk about telephone calls when a problem arises, letters to inform parents about a particular sanction or a notice in a bulletin that might or might not be read. Some colleagues mention having pastoral add-on sessions when academic events take place. Some schools run classes for parents to enable them to support their children at home or organise school events to engage the whole family. These are all valuable events that serve a particular purpose and contribute to pastoral engagement, although not all of these interactions can be described as proactive.

Community building and pastoral parental engagement must be a priority for the school and senior leaders must act to secure commitment from staff and communicate their vision regarding proactive pastoral engagement. Pastoral engagement requires commitment and creativity: it might be that some groups of parents need personalised approaches to ensure a positive response. As strategic leaders of their organisations responsible for the values of the school that underpin culture, policy and procedures, it is important that governors offer support, connecting with the parental body they serve. It is not about ticking boxes and having parental representation on the board; it is about actively communicating with parents and carers and ensuring that this communication informs the board's decision-making. Being proactive in liaising with parents is important, as it will enhance parental confidence and trust in the organisation. However, it is quite acceptable for governors not to agree with the parents on certain matters and act in the best interests of pupils. The National Governance Association (NGA) recommends that governing boards follow 'the seven Nolan principles of public life, which includes openness and accountability, features essential to engaging with parents. Without these characteristics, your governing board is not only doing a disservice to the parent community but also to themselves.'

A model for parental engagement

Looking at parental engagement processes, it is also useful to mention a parental engagement model designed by Piotrowska et al. (2017): CAPE. It consists of:

Connect: recruitment and enrolment – this involves ensuring that the reach of the programme is sufficient to connect with parents and encourage them to enrol.

Attend: retention – this refers to the continuous presence of parents at physical events or sessions, or regularly logging in to online programmes.

Participate: involvement – this goes beyond simply attendance and means active involvement from the parents, for example the completion of home practice or being active in group discussions.

Enact: implementation – parents put into practice newly learned strategies and techniques.

The researchers warn that 'the first three model stages (Connect, Attend, and Participate) are known to be predicted by a set of factors including family characteristics (for example, a parent's age, socioeconomic status, economic stress and family structure), child characteristics (for example, age, gender and difficulties profile), family processes (for example, parental mental health, interparental conflict and relationship quality, family or household chaos, and the current level of parenting skills), contextual factors (for example, beliefs about parenting roles, cultural factors, parental personality, and help-seeking beliefs), and organisational factors (for example, therapist factors, programme help interface, access and availability factors).'

The researchers also distinguish between recognised *direct* and *indirect* participation. 'Direct Participation refers to active commitment, physical presence, and involvement with the programme materials, whereas [Indirect Participation] refers to acquiring information from other sources especially in the context of a parenting team, i.e. one parent may register and directly engage with a programme (in person or online) and later teach and train their partner in the use of relevant strategies.' Active parental participation is likely to lead to competent and consistent enactment of the presented principles or strategies, which would in turn lead to positive changes in the families and eventually improved wellbeing.

CAPE is a useful model to bear in mind when working on improving parental engagement as it provides a framework and structure to work with that makes it more manageable to assess parental engagement. The last stage 'Enact' is difficult to operationalise and measure as it is when changes in parenting should take place. There might be a number of obstacles that prevent enactment from taking place, for example, family environment, differences and inconsistencies in parenting styles, or lack of confidence or time. It would depend on the relationship between school and parents as to whether they would feel able to be honest, and disclose and discuss this type of information.

Strategies to secure pastoral parental engagement

I am now going to offer a number of strategies tried and tested by me and by many of my colleagues over the years. They are not a magical solution to suddenly securing pastoral parental engagement; this is just a starting point. It is important to discuss and determine what would work in your own context, in your own unique environment, for you as a pastoral leader.

1. Include a welcome from your pastoral team at the start of every school year to establish clear channels of pastoral communication. This can be done via a welcome email, an information pack for new families or a school calendar, for example.

2. Establish parental focus groups and encourage parents to organise events, which gives them a greater sense of ownership.

3. Establish the active role of parent governor to bring together parents, governors and staff.

4. Identify parents who are already engaged and who might have ideas of how to engage other parents.

5. Identify and address families' practical and psychological barriers effectively before a particular event or intervention. For example, due to the change in parent–child relationships through secondary school (with increased autonomy and a desire to spend time with peers during the adolescent years), parents might assume that their engagement is not as important any more. It might also be that parents are not able to travel to school for a variety of reasons. Using a school minibus to bring parents to school could be a solution.

6. Allow parents to choose the themes or names for pastoral events run by the school.

7. Involve student ambassadors in communication with parents.

8. Invite parents to deliver PSHE lessons if they have relevant skills or experience. In my experience, some engaging financial or volunteering sessions were delivered by parents who were working in these fields.

9. Engage parents in promoting diversity – educating the school community about their culture and traditions as part of the school's diversity celebration events.

10. If parents are not going to come to school, take the school to parents: it might be worth exploring an idea of arranging an event away from school – in community centres, cafes or cultural buildings – thus removing the barriers that may be caused by the school buildings.

However we choose to enhance parental engagement, it is important that we establish and promote an open culture that nurtures relationships and takes into account parental views on the school values, ethos and wellbeing vision that underpin proactive pastoral care.

Reflections

1. What practical barriers to engagement might parents be experiencing?

_____

_____

_____

_____

_____

_____

2. What psychological barriers to engagement might parents be experiencing?

_____

_____

_____

_____

_____

_____

3. How could these barriers be broken down?

_____

_____

_____

_____

_____

_____

4. What are you already doing towards building proactive pastoral engagement in these four areas that underpin wellbeing?

Physical and mental health	Emotional health	Social health	Spiritual health

5. What else can be done by staff and by governors? Add ideas to the columns using a different-coloured pen.

_____

_____

_____

6 Pastoral curriculum: PSHE

Overview

This chapter will:

- look at five main elements of planning a PSHE programme to support proactive pastoral care:
  - content
  - structure
  - learning and teaching
  - delivery
  - assessment.

PSHE lessons are an obvious means of providing directed time for students to develop skills that are essential parts of proactive pastoral care and form part of character education, as mentioned in an earlier chapter.

As leaders and teachers, at any stage of our career, whichever post we hold, one thing remains a constant: we must always have our pupils' interests at heart. What do we want for our pupils? We want to see our young people happy, mentally and physically healthy, and safe. We want our young people to be resilient, proactive and independent. We want them to acquire knowledge as well as develop their moral compass to empower them to make the right choices in their personal and academic lives. A well-structured PSHE programme is essential to supporting this.

Planning a PSHE programme

So, how do we create a sustainable, preventative PSHE programme that challenges and promotes the personal development of our young people throughout their school life? Working with schools, as well as within my own context, I have identified five main aspects that need to be taken into account during the planning process:

1. content

2. structure

3. learning and teaching

4. delivery

5. assessment.

I will look at each in turn.

Content

Starting with the content enables you to look at the big picture. What do our young people need to know? What statutory aspects are there? The statutory requirements are a good place to begin. The Department for Education in England has statutory content and guidance on drug education, financial education, RSE, and the importance of physical activity and diet for a healthy lifestyle. The Department for Education (2020) states that schools should use PSHE lessons to build on this where appropriate.

I have identified five main strands based on available research and advice:

- **Education and finances:** study skills, revision, university applications, higher education, apprenticeships, careers, economic and financial literacy, budgeting, debt and taxes, loans and so on.

- **Safety:** PREVENT, road safety, first aid, e-safety, child sexual exploitation, female genital mutilation (FGM) and so on.

- **Personal identity and relationships:** values, character education, friendship, family, RSE, diversity and discrimination, consent, abusive relationships, and so on.

- **Wellbeing and healthy living:** mental and emotional health, coping strategies, healthy diet, alcohol, drugs, energy drinks, gaming and gambling, digital wellbeing, and so on.

- **Citizenship and charity:** the political system, voting, Parliament, the legal and justice system, fundraising, volunteering, and so on.

These strands apply to all year groups at a primary or secondary level, although some of the sub-topics will be relevant only to certain age groups. Having the strands enables you to design a clear structure of the programme, while the sub-topics allow for some flexibility within the strands to cater for specific age-related issues. Within the ever-changing landscape of pastoral care, this is a strong foundation to build on in the years to come.

Structure

When structuring a PSHE programme, it is advisable to adopt a 'spiral learning model' (Bruner, 1960). Bruner's theory is that pupils of any age can understand even the most complex of material if it's properly structured and presented. He advocates that pupils revisit topics several times throughout their schooling, with the complexity of the content increasing each time and links being made between new learning and prior learning. Using this model to structure a PSHE curriculum ensures that the topics are revisited and covered at a greater depth throughout school years, allowing for a fluid transfer of knowledge. It also helps to ensure that you don't have stand-alone lessons to tick certain boxes, but allow for the in-depth development of the topics for the long-term benefit of our young people. For example, at the start of secondary school, the relationships strand is covered through the topic of friendships and family, then recapped and further extended the following year by looking at relationships between boyfriends and girlfriends. The table below shows how a simplified framework for a RSE programme might work in a secondary school from Years 7 to 11.

	Year 7	Year 8	Year 9	Year 10	Year 11
Relationships	Different types of families; healthy and toxic friendships, etc.	Relationships between boyfriends and girlfriends; communicating in relationships, etc.	Gender identity; relationships online; sexting, etc.	Values: healthy and unhealthy relationships; consent	Marriage; parenting; abuse; honour-based violence, etc.
Sex education	Puberty	Menstrual wellbeing; conception	STIs; contraception	Intimate sexual relationships; accessing sexual health services	Sexual consent; pregnancy; miscarriage

This is not a comprehensive scheme of work; it is used here to demonstrate what a spiral learning model might look like. We come from different contexts, and children should be in the centre of our planning: it is their development rather than age that needs to be given a greater priority.

Another point to consider is the importance of having a whole-school overview of what is being delivered by other departments. For example, topics such as stereotypes, gender, nudity, beliefs, and so on might be covered in art, while topics like prostitution and marriage in the ancient world might be covered in Latin. History teachers might touch upon topics of friendships, peer pressure, gangs and sex, while RE teachers are likely to dwell on values, marriage and abortion.

Learning and teaching

Although we are not delivering academic material in PSHE lessons, the planning of the lessons must be approached with the same rigour as any other lesson. First, we must aim to ensure that PSHE has the same status as any academic subject:

- PSHE should be given enough curriculum time to cater for all year groups.
- The quality of teaching and learning should be evaluated by the person responsible for PSHE and by the senior leadership team.
- Pupil progress and work should be monitored throughout the year.
- Like any other lesson, PSHE lessons should have a clearly defined learning trajectory captured and evidenced in a lesson plan.
- PSHE (the pastoral curriculum) should form part of the appraisal process.

Second, we should provide a breadth of learning opportunities and ensure that our teaching caters for the needs of all of our pupils. Differentiation in PSHE can be approached in many different ways. As I have pointed out before, we must take into account where pupils are in terms of their development to ensure that we meet their developmental needs. It is also important to remember that there are many practical methods of differentiation that can be applied to any teaching context. For example, it is easy to fill the opening five minutes of the lesson by providing text such as key phrases, facts and goals, but straight away this disadvantages pupils who are struggling with literacy acquisition. An easy solution is to replace the text with an aural, oral or kinaesthetic activity. This is a broader approach to differentiation as we are moving from singling out and explicitly supporting particular pupils towards making our classrooms truly inclusive.

If external speakers are invited to deliver a particular session, it would be good practice for them to send you their presentations in advance, so that you could adjust the lessons before or after to reinforce the learning and ensure continuity for a greater impact. As you know your children better than your speaker, it is good practice to provide a brief overview of the group, what has been covered before, goals for the session, and so on. Speakers are contributing to your overall programme, so it is important to communicate as much as appropriate in advance.

Delivery

The delivery of PSHE lessons depends on the school structure and budget. Some schools choose the option of having specialised teachers delivering the lessons, whereas others assign this task to tutors; some schools will have a mixed structure, when specialised teachers will deliver more sensitive topics, while other schools might assign tutors to a specialist team delivering one of the content areas to a specific year group. Each of these types of delivery has its advantages and disadvantages. The form tutor delivery can be problematic and lower the credibility of the subject. The obvious advantage of having specialised teachers is the depth of knowledge and consistency; tutors in the same year group might have different levels of knowledge or confidence to provide consistency across the board. Having a specialist team empowers tutors to have more ownership and encourages them to research a particular area extensively, which builds up their confidence and deepens their knowledge and understanding.

The main thing to bear in mind is that, like in any academic subject, delivery needs to be monitored formally and informally. It can be part of appraisal or performance management. It can be part of coaching observation or a more official observation carried out by a trained member of the pastoral team. And although gathering evidence is part of the monitoring process, the main purpose is to ensure consistency of delivery within and across various year groups.

Assessment

It is important to remember that 'teaching isn't just about delivering a curriculum with its achievement of measurable outcomes' (Goddard et al., 2013). The outcomes of the learning that has taken place during PSHE lessons may not be evident until our young people leave the school, although one thing is clear: in order to be successful learners, pupils need regular opportunities to reflect and establish what they have learnt and how they could develop their knowledge further.

Although it is tricky to assess some of the less factual content of PSHE lessons, there is a lot of scope for formative assessment, especially peer-assessment. For example, when presented with various relationship scenarios, pupils have an opportunity to assess the behaviour and actions presented against values or moral standards and beliefs, with the aim of effecting behaviour change.

Self-assessment can be used effectively during reflection activities. You could try the following questions:

- Have you learnt anything new today?
- Have you developed any new skills?
- Do you think differently about this issue after today's session?

These opportunities for assessment are not necessarily formalised, as in other subjects; rather, they should become an integral and natural part of the learning process. You can also use formative and summative assessment to assess different types of knowledge in the PSHE curriculum:

- Formative assessment activities would be more open-ended and used when dealing with values and attitudes or the development of personal skills.
- Summative assessment can be used to establish factual knowledge – for example, to assess pupils' understanding of different types of contraception or the classification of drugs.

The whole structure of the PSHE programme should be based on the baseline assessment carried out by the person responsible for the PSHE provision to ensure that the lessons are relevant and appropriately developed for each year group.

*

A good PSHE programme should be proactive in nature and help to pre-empt possible unpleasant events or issues in the future. The value of a strong pastoral curriculum cannot be underestimated: a school's academic programme won't function effectively if children are ill, tired or anxious or have found themselves in difficult situations at home or with their friends: 'anxiety is a key block to learning. It can prevent the imprint on the brain' (McCulloch, 2008, quoted in Carpenter, 2020).

It is important to remember, however, that for the programme to be successfully embedded in the school curriculum, it is vital to establish a wellbeing culture, as I have mentioned before, and to secure staff's commitment to the pastoral curriculum. Many initiatives and programmes do not bring sustainable change as they are not aligned with the school structure or, most importantly, schools are trying to establish something without tackling the main issue: their culture.

Reflections

1. What are your school values?

_____

_____

_____

2. How does your pastoral curriculum reinforce those values?

_____

_____

_____

3. How does your pastoral curriculum support these four areas of wellbeing?

Physical and mental health	Emotional health	Social health	Spiritual health

4. What are the obstacles to the delivery of a successful PSHE programme? How can you address them? Who can support you?

_____

_____

_____

5. How often do staff receive pastoral training?

_____

_____

_____

6. Is the pastoral curriculum included in staff's appraisal or performance management form?

_____

_____

_____

7 E-safety: thriving in a digital world

> **Overview**
>
> This chapter will:
>
> - consider the benefits and the potential dangers of technology, with a focus on social media
> - discuss unhealthy digital habits and the influence parents can have on these
> - examine how schools can be more proactive about key aspects of e-safety, including:
>   - digital security
>   - digital lifestyle
>   - digital relationships.

As we have seen in Chapter 2, 'inconsistent use of definitions, indicators, and measures of well-being has created a confusing and contradictory research base' (Pollard and Lee, 2003). Digital wellbeing is a field that is even more challenging to study, not just because of the contradictory research around wellbeing more generally but also because not enough research has been dedicated to the impact of technology on different areas of wellbeing. Philip Brey (2012), a professor of the philosophy of technology, also adds that, 'In spite of the pervasive role of technology in modern society and contemporary life, very little research on well-being has focused on technology. Technology hardly registers as a topic in positive psychology or happiness economics, and in philosophy the situation is not much better.'

Although digital wellbeing has been neglected in the academic literature, we cannot ignore the fact that nowadays not only do young people have the pressures of the real world to deal with, but the digital world has also become an integral part of their lives. Professor Brigitte Jordan (2009) notes that 'a central consideration revolves around the observation that a growing number of people now live in a hybrid world where the boundaries between what is physical (or actual) and what is digital (or electronic) continue to fade.' People now inhabit a world where their identity, experiences and life possibilities 'begin to integrate physical and virtual facets of existence, so that consciousness is to some extent shared between an offline physical and online virtual self'. Although this point of view has been debated, it has become clearer during the COVID-19 pandemic, with schools' reliance on digital tools, that the way we do things has changed significantly. Anyone who has pastoral responsibilities in a school must consider the impact this may have on the wellbeing of their pupils.

Social media

Online interactions have been of great concern to many professionals working with young people, as pupils tend to engage in many unhealthy interactions on social media platforms. We know that social interaction is essential to a person's wellbeing, and social media does help to enable this, but young people are not necessarily equipped to cope with the complexities of the digital world. James et al. (2017) conclude that 'Social connection is a fundamental human need. Children and teenagers develop social skills as they grow and practice strategies to fulfil their needs for family, friendship, and intimacy. Increasingly, these strategies leverage networked technologies. Consequently, today's adolescents require specific supports and coping skills to prepare them for a digitally connected society.'

It is also fair to say that young people require more and more support as their digital interactions are becoming increasingly complex with the development of technology. Lomanowska and Guitton (2012) point to 'highly immersive three-dimensional virtual worlds' that have become a 'popular medium for human social interactions'. This technology allows users to experience 'multimodal sensory engagement' and 'an immersive graphical representation of physical space where users can interact via avatars.'

On the one hand, due to these constant changes in digital interactions, it is important for young people to keep acquiring skills to enable them to keep up with and manage digital communication. On the other hand, as the brain 'shifts its focus toward new technological skills, it drifts away from fundamental social skills, such as reading facial expressions during conversation or grasping the emotional context of a subtle gesture.' (Small and Vorgan, 2008)

There exist a number of misconceptions and differences of opinions around teenagers and their use of technology. Writer and inventor Marc Prensky (2001) distinguishes between 'digital natives' and 'digital immigrants', claiming that young people are 'native speakers of the digital language of computers, video games and the Internet.' Similarly Professor Gary Small and his wife Gigi Vorgan (2008) warn that 'we are witnessing the beginning of a deeply divided *brain gap* between younger and older minds'. At the same time, Dr Jakob Nielsen (2005) claims that 'teenagers are not in fact superior Web geniuses who can use anything a site throws at them.' In his research, adults achieved a higher success rate than teenagers in the tasks set. The main factors were insufficient reading skills displayed by teenagers, their less sophisticated research strategies, and much lower patience levels. None of these factors would come as a total surprise to teachers.

The attitudes of adults towards social media throughout the last few years have often been influenced by sensational articles in the media. For example, social media has been linked to increased risks of depression (Miller), and teenagers who use the internet excessively have been compared to compulsive gamblers and cocaine users (Bowater, 2012). Although attitudes have started to change (COVID-19 has made social media one of the main ways for us to communicate), even now if you were to run an internet search for 'social media and…', the picture you would get is quite bleak:

SEARCH: social media and

RESULTS: social media and mental health
social media and relationships
social media and depression

It's no wonder therefore that technology and the use of technology have been at the forefront of many wellbeing debates.

The dual nature of technology

Let's consider further research into this area. Taylor (1991) claims that 'the dominant place of technology is... thought to have contributed to the narrowing and flattening of our lives. People have spoken of a loss of resonance, depth, or richness in our human surroundings.' Darvin (2016) highlighted the dual nature of technology by stating that on one hand 'technology destroys our ability to communicate and interact with others meaningfully and is responsible for shorter attention spans, language deterioration and erosion of privacy. On the other hand, utopian views of technology attribute progress and change to technology and regard it as something that will transform the world ultimately for the better.' Focusing on the positives of technology, James et al. (2017) add that apps, games and wearable devices, alongside online social reinforcement and feedback, can support healthy behaviour and habits, such as exercise and reflection. At the same time, some of those devices could be dangerous for people with eating disorders.

Unhealthy habits and the influence of parents

Many of our young people are surrounded by technology from the minute they wake up until they go to bed. In her book *Digital Parenting*, Neelam Parmar (2017) claims that our children 'are able to switch between devices, applications and social media throughout the day, without even realising what they are doing. For many of them, digital life is just life.' Research conducted by Statistic Brain and quoted by Morgan (2018) shows that '1,325,000,000 people were using YouTube; 300 hours of content were being uploaded per minute; 4,950,000,000 videos were viewed per day; and over 10,000 videos had been seen over a billion times.' Nowadays you don't need to be in front of the computer to be using the internet; mobile devices let our children go online when they are at home, when they are at school and when they are commuting. According to research into students using mobile devices at night, conducted by the Headmasters' and Headmistresses' Conference (HMC) and Digital Awareness UK (2016), 'a third (32%) of these students' parents are not aware that they check their mobile device after going to bed.' It would have been useful to find out why these parents are unaware; is it a lack of control or knowledge or both? Interestingly, the research offers some more revealing data: 'over a third (36%) of children say they have asked their parents to stop checking their mobile devices. Almost half of them (46%) say it makes no difference when they do so. However, under 10% of parents thought their time spent on devices was concerning their children.' Moreover, '21% of parents report being online for 6–10 hours during an average working day and 37% say they are online between 3 and 5 hours a day at weekends. 5% are online between ten and 15 hours at weekends.' According to the same research, 68 per cent of students say that using their mobile devices at night affects their school work and 45 per cent of students admit they check their mobile device after going to bed. Of those, 23 per cent check their mobile device more than ten times a night. So, the data clearly highlights some unhealthy habits, and parents are often advised to turn off Wi-Fi and keep gadgets downstairs.

But it's not always as simple as that. In fact, some suggest that depriving children from the internet and banning it at home is 'tantamount to child abuse' (Petter, 2018). Professor Sonia Livingstone (2017) encourages us to 'become critical readers of popular claims about media harm... we should ask why the finger of blame is always pointed at the media rather than other likely causes (including violence against women, or problems linked to growing inequality or precarity).'

And what about adults who are responsible for safeguarding their children's wellbeing at home? In their book *The Digital Invasion*, Archibald Hart and Sylvia Hart Frejd (2013) suggest that 'many parents may no longer be good models for their own children and have become as digitally dependent as the younger generation.' We talk to parents about the difficulties of digital parenting, yet we rarely look at adult behaviour in the digital world or consider how it affects the habits that children form. For most adults, however, it is still possible to distinguish between the two worlds quite clearly, as we know what it used to be like before the digital takeover happened. After all, it was only in 1991 that the web became publicly available. It wasn't until 2004 that Facebook was founded, followed by YouTube in 2005, Twitter in 2006 and Instagram in 2010. The first iPhone was released in 2007, and the first Wi-Fi-enabled iPad came in 2010.

But there's no denying that these fairly recent developments have had a profound effect on our lives, especially in terms of speed. The speed of communication and decision-making, the speed of sharing news, the speed of apps appearing, reaching their peak and vanishing into thin air. That pace is the norm for children now, while many adults are still adapting to that lifestyle, forming healthy or unhealthy habits in the process. Every family is unique, everybody's circumstances are unique, and we are dealing with the real and digital lives in our unique way. It is important that, as adults, we are honest with ourselves about our own digital habits, as digital parenting is not just about setting controls, switching off the Wi-Fi, talking about the importance of real-life communication and then going on our own devices thinking that our job is done. Digital parenting is also about modelling and showing what healthy really looks like in practice.

As e-safety co-ordinator in a large 3–18 independent school, I was often required to deal with the aftermath of digital incidents that had taken place at home, when pupils had been in their parents' care, often caused by the parents' lack of knowledge or understanding of the digital world, their lack of confidence when it comes to technology or a simple lack of time or ignorance. McAffee's survey conducted in 2010 and quoted by Parmar (2017) confirmed that 'two out of three parents are ignorant of their children's Internet activities'. This brings us back to Prensky's (2001) idea of 'digital natives' and 'digital immigrants'. However, I cannot completely agree with these categories as they appear to be over-simplistic and, as a result, lacking many nuances. Just because the younger generation is growing up with all the technology and social media that is accessible to them does not mean that they will be able to or will want to access it. Helsper (2008) also warns that 'the digital natives discourse prevents young people from seeking advice and may cause them to under-estimate online dangers.' It also seems that by this division we promote the deficit model – as an older generation, as 'immigrants', we will never be able to compete with the 'natives'; we will never be good enough.

Proactive e-safety in schools

It has been my conviction for a long time that we are often reactive to what is happening in the digital world. We fail to tackle the root of the problem, often trying to teach e-safety as an add-on and picking one or two specific aspects, without fully understanding the enormity and complexity of this area. For example, many schools manage the use of mobiles or ban them altogether in line with their policies, although accidents would still happen in such areas as toilets and changing rooms. It is clear that there is no consensus regarding the use of mobiles at schools, and as it is left to the headteacher to make the final decision, it is important to take into consideration the school's unique context. The research in this area has not been conclusive or helpful. A project carried out by Louis-Philippe Beland (2015) and Richard Murphy at Birmingham, London, Leicester and Manchester schools showed that 'following a ban on phone use, student test scores improve by 6.41 per cent of a standard deviation'. However, the researchers stress that 'there are no significant gains in student performance if a ban is not widely complied with'. At the same time, a 2014 report written by Stanford professors Linda Darling-Hammond and Shelley Goldman, together with doctoral student Molly B. Zielezinski, found that technology – when implemented properly – can produce significant gains in student achievement and boost engagement.

However, whatever the school policy is, a large number of incidents will take place outside of school walls and hours, often in the comfort of our pupils' homes.

In order to be proactive in managing e-safety in our schools, it is vital to educate our young people and communicate closely with their parents. So, what information should we be communicating? My first suggestion is to break down the vast topic of e-safety into three manageable areas: digital security, digital lifestyle and digital relationships.

1. Digital security

Digital security can be divided into three further areas to enable us to approach this topic from different angles, taking into account a variety of tools families and young people could utilise to protect their online identity.

Personal security

This is the area that children should be empowered to be fully responsible for: keeping their passwords safe and managing their privacy settings and safety features of websites, as well as using or deactivating location settings or GPS on websites, apps or games.

According to a YouGov poll conducted for the NSPCC, only 28 per cent of parents had actually mentioned privacy settings to their children and 20 per cent had discussed location settings.

There are three things I would advise parents to consider to empower their children to take responsibility for their personal security:

1. Be a role model. Have you got your own privacy settings under control? Use your own behaviour to guide your child.
2. Talk, talk, talk. In the same way we talk to children about keeping safe in the real world, we should talk about online safety and personal security in the digital world too.

3. Encourage and praise. Many young people I speak to admit that conversations with their parents about the digital world are often quite negative. If we notice positive digital behaviours, we should acknowledge and encourage them too.

Home security

Parental controls can be useful. You can find some tips and strategies on a number of websites. Internet Matters is one of them. However, it is important to remember that all families are unique and operate in different ways. When a child visits a friend or stays over for a sleepover, their family is trusting them to behave with integrity, irrespective of the presence or absence of parental controls. Instead of controlling, we should aim to empower our children, give them ownership of their decisions and instil a sense of responsibility.

Social media platform security

Parents can find information on various platforms through NSPCC Net Aware, a site run in partnership with O2. However, the reality is that there is a large number of social media apps and websites appearing all the time. Some are more dangerous than others; it is impossible to collate a comprehensive list as there are so many. The good thing is that they disappear as fast as they appear. However, once again, as we are not able to guarantee their security, we are trusting our children to have a well-developed moral compass to ensure they stay safe online.

2. Digital lifestyle

Interrupted sleep, exposure to the blue light from smartphones and tablets, second screening (using two screens simultaneously), fear of missing out (FOMO), mood swings and anxiety are just some of the common problems associated with an unhealthy digital lifestyle.

Apps such as WhatsApp make it harder for children to break the vicious circle of unhealthy engagement. Children can be added to a WhatsApp group without their permission and leaving a group secretly is impossible, unless they pluck up the courage to delete a WhatsApp group on their device completely without leaving it.

COVID-19 has played a major role in restricting our face-to-face activities and transferring our lives online. Despite all the advice we have given over the years, we are now forced to study, work and socialise online. During the pandemic and beyond, what can pastoral leaders and parents do to empower young people to lead a healthy digital lifestyle? Education remains key: pastoral leaders should persist in being proactive and educating pupils and their parents. We must aim to balance highlighting risks with dwelling on the positives. Here are three ideas to consider:

1. Parents could encourage their children to establish healthy routines and habits at home, which include creating social media rules, turning off notifications, having phone-free zones, or getting involved in activities away from screens: doing something creative or having a physical exercise break. In the pandemic, we can use digital tools to regain some sort of control of our lives: making plans for the future, 'meeting up' with friends or shopping. Remember: control the digital world, do not let the digital world control you.

2. Increasing our self-awareness helps us to become more mindful rather than doing things on autopilot. Both pastoral leaders and parents could help young people gain clarity and understanding of their actions with the following questions: why am I reaching for my device? Why am I posting this? Am I looking for inclusion, reassurance, or maybe I need some positive comments to make me feel better? Right now, am I making my life better or worse by using technology? What am I trying to replace or avoid? We must acknowledge that all screen time is not equal: understanding the why behind our use of technology is important.

3. Pastoral leaders and parents can play a vital role in encouraging young people to create their own happy digital world in alignment with their interests and values: blocking the bullies, communicating with people who make their life better, not worse, and listening to music that boosts their mood are just some possible strategies.

3. Digital relationships

The nature and complexity of online incidents vary greatly: anything from a pupil being ignored in a chat room to online bullying (including fake profiles and stalking), sexting, pornography, grooming and radicalisation.

Pastoral leaders spend a lot of time being reactive in dealing with the aftermath of digital relationships going wrong. But what if we were to instead focus on preparing our young people for the digital world and on empowering them to create and sustain positive relationships? If we can teach pupils not to engage with unhealthy situations or relationships online in the first place, then we can stop being reactive and start taking a more proactive approach. Here are three steps in the right direction.

Develop a moral compass and nurture strong values

Healthy behaviours are underpinned by values and morals. This is especially true when forming positive digital behaviours and healthy relationships, as we should expect our young people to uphold the same standard of behaviour online as in real life, acting with integrity at all times. This is something that does not need technical knowledge, but would require a strong school culture and positive nurturing relationships at home where communication is positive and underpinned by trust, honesty and support.

Nurture mental health and wellbeing

It is when we are feeling vulnerable that we are more likely to engage in unhealthy relationships in our conscious or unconscious search to satisfy basic human needs, such as the need for belonging and acceptance and the need to feel valued and secure. Empowering young people to look after their mental health and wellbeing and creating secure environments at school and at home should be our number one priority.

Develop awareness

In order to respond to risk, pupils need to be able to recognise it. It is important for pupils to be aware and mindful of the following signs of unhealthy relationships:

- feeling the pressure to change or do something you don't want to do
- feeling you have to hide things or be secretive
- having to justify your actions
- making it difficult to maintain relationships with family or friends
- lack of common friends
- lack of respect for each other's family
- verbal, emotional or physical abuse (using the 'silent treatment', disappearing, name-calling, and so on)
- controlling behaviours (excessive calling, texting, stalking, lack of privacy, and so on).

Most of these signs can be easily applied to real-life situations as well as the digital world (we will look at this in more detail in our next section). Parents and schools need to be working in partnership to educate young people about healthy and unhealthy relationships and how to recognise the signs. At the same time, although educating about the risk is a necessary preventative measure, it is not enough. It is important that young people act on this awareness. In order to do this, they need to act from the position of mental and emotional strength and be prepared to break unhealthy attachments.

Although the picture is quite bleak when it comes to social media, we should avoid focusing solely on the negative narrative. Social media is also a great tool to connect, to promote your work, to do research and to learn new things. We should aim to flip the narrative when teaching about the digital world: it is our responsibility not just to teach about the dangers, but to empower our young people to become responsible digital citizens and to use technology for good, to make a difference and to leave a positive and inspiring mark on the world.

Reflections

1. Would you describe your school's approach to e-safety as reactive or proactive? Why?

    _____

    _____

    _____

2. What are you already doing in terms of e-safety to support each of the wellbeing areas? Which areas do you need to work on? Think about digital safety, digital lifestyle and digital relationships.

Physical and mental health	Emotional health	Social health	Spiritual health

3. If you were to design a training course for staff and parents around e-safety, what would you include in it?

    _____

    _____

    _____

4. What positive elements about technology do you include in your curriculum?

_____

_____

_____

8 Embedding relationships and sex education (RSE)

> ## Overview
>
> This chapter will:
>
> - explain the importance of relationships education, including self-care and self-awareness
> - provide advice on teaching about positive and negative relationships
> - offer a set of discussion questions to support relationships education
> - consider how to help pupils turn theory into application
> - explore sex education and how to teach about healthy sexual relationships
> - discuss inclusive RSE.

There has been a lot of debate about relationships and sex education (RSE) for a long time. As I write in the academic year 2020/2021, we are now at the stage when schools would have prepared their RSE policies and considered compulsory requirements identified by the government. The purpose of this section is not to debate the decisions made, but to provide a pathway to ensure that RSE is fully embedded in the curriculum and does not become a tick-box exercise to ensure compliance. If we are focusing solely on compliance and inspection, we are not likely to do it justice. Let's dig deeper.

Relationships education

As social beings, we form different relationships throughout our lifetime, so it comes as no surprise that the word 'relationships' comes before 'sex' in the new title of this curriculum area. We start forming relationships from a very young age; our relationship with the caregiver or caregivers is an important one. You will have heard the phrase 'attachment theory'. Simply put, it explains how the parent–child relationship emerges and influences subsequent social, emotional and cognitive development. Attachment theory originates from the work of John Bowlby (1958), who later described attachment as a 'lasting psychological connectedness between human beings' (Bowlby, 1969). The central theme of attachment is that if the primary caregiver is available and responsive to the child's needs, this empowers the child to develop a sense of security, which then allows the child to explore the world. Fonagy et al. (2002, quoted in Holmes, 2005) suggest that the emotional and physical proximity that attachment ensures equips infants with the capacity to understand themselves and those around them. When we are looking at family as one of the RSE topics, it is important to ensure that we take into consideration all pupils – those who have secure and insecure attachments – as they will look at the topic through the lens of their personal experiences. It is our responsibility to create an inclusive and safe environment to allow for these topics to be taught and discussed, but it can only be done if staff have sufficient pastoral knowledge. It is the responsibility of the person who is leading on proactive pastoral care to make certain that the staff have the training required to ensure that they can teach relationship topics with sensitivity and notice potential issues.

As our young people go through school and mature, their relationships with parents and friends will change and they will develop new relationships: with new teachers, new classmates or boyfriends and girlfriends. However, the most important relationship they will have in life is with themselves as it 'sets the tone for every other relationship' they have (Holden, 2020). This is something that we often do not cover explicitly in lessons but it is essential that we do as part of proactive pastoral care.

Self-care and self-awareness

Self-care starts with self-awareness. To ascertain levels of self-awareness, try asking the following questions:

- Do you know yourself as a human being?
- Are you kind to yourself?
- What makes you happy?
- What makes you sad?
- What are you saying to yourself?
- Would you say it to someone else?
- How often do you focus on your inner world?
- Do you have a sound understanding of what wellbeing is and how you can cultivate it?

Once our young people have a greater degree of self-awareness and our staff are equipped with the necessary knowledge, the teaching of the relationship component of RSE becomes easier, as you will have already built the strong foundations needed to truly embed RSE into your pastoral provision.

Teaching about positive and negative relationships

We often approach the topic of relationships from a negative point of view: toxic relationships, domestic violence, and so on. There is no doubt that our young people need this knowledge: this material will enhance their awareness and enable them to recognise the signs of unhealthy relationships. It needs to be taught with sensitivity as we may not know who might be going through similar experiences; as a result you could witness an increase in disclosures. At the same time, young people need to see stable, happy, loving relationships and look at how they are created and nurtured. They need to have positive role models: something to aspire and aim for.

A lot of attention has been given to the sex component of the RSE curriculum, but we need to remember that sex is only part of any healthy relationship (whether it's heterosexual, pansexual, homosexual, and so on), alongside trust, understanding, honesty, teamwork and communication. One of the best lessons I have had was around the word 'love' and how it means different things to different people, and how we express love to each other in different ways that can sometimes be misunderstood by another person and lead to arguments. By any means, I am not trying to ignore the sex part of RSE; my only point is to show that we have more things that unite us as human beings, as we share human values that underpin any healthy relationship and any family structure (same-sex, foster, single parent families, and so on). Respecting other people's views, honest communication and having freedom to make your own choices are all attributes of healthy relationships. Before pupils become sexually active, it is important to introduce the topic of consent: assumptions relating to consent, the right to withdraw consent, the capacity to consent (for example, alcohol or drug use can impede our decision-making).

Discussion questions around relationships

The following questions can be useful in group or class discussion:

- Define the value of love (think about family, friends and other relationships).
- How can we show love for each other?
- Design your own checklist for love in alignment with your values.

- What values guide family life (the word 'family' is used here to refer to all different types of families).

- 'The family is an arena in which virtually the entire range of human experiences can take place. Warfare, love, violence, tenderness, honesty, deceit, private property, communal sharing, power, manipulation, informed consent, formal status hierarchies, egalitarian decision-making – all can be found within the setting of the family.' (Leichter, 1974) How can you set boundaries in a relationship?

- Healthy relationships take work. How ready and willing are you to commit to building a relationship, whether it's a friendship, a relationship with a family member, a romantic relationship or any other type of relationship?

- There is no doubt that your relationships will be tested at one time or another. How can you ensure they withstand the storm?

The last two questions are very important as they put the emphasis on the young person. Proactive pastoral care is about empowerment; it's not about learning the signs of healthy and unhealthy relationships and reciting them from memory. It is about young people's values, wellbeing state, environment, social circles and many other factors.

Theory versus application

There is a huge gap between knowing right from wrong and applying that knowledge, as a young person can be influenced by various internal and external circumstances. Human behaviour is a complex area and is one that fascinates me; I am captivated by people and their stories. The topic of relationships cannot be covered fully in one chapter, but I will attempt to provide some food for thought as it will support your pastoral planning. Parrish (2014) states that 'The discussion of behaviour entails a complex array of patterns and differences… Behaviours range from measurable, observable manifestations of our internal states, to impulsive reactions to fear or pain, to intentional or unintentional responses to an array of factors.

Those factors may include age, gender, health, socio-economic circumstances, sexual orientation, and intellectual differences, among others.' Neave (2008) also researched how hormones affect behaviour and how they can influence brain structure and function. Other researchers specifically focused on understanding the teenage brain and the behaviour of teenagers (see, for example, Jensen, 2015 and Blakemore, 2018). With so much research, so many variables and not enough time allocated to the pastoral curriculum, what can we do to help young people bridge the previously mentioned gap between theoretical knowledge and its application?

Throughout the years, the same three things have been identified over and over again to help with this:

1. **Relationships between teachers and pupils:** Caring connections could be an important protective factor for vulnerable pupils.

2. **Pastoral structures that are inclusive and proactive:** These structures allow pupils to fail in a safe environment and put their values into practice.

3. **Strong school values that unite the whole community, from the cleaners to the headteacher:** Schools are extremely hierarchical organisations and it is vital that no matter where the staff are according to the hierarchy structure, they feel ownership for embedding school values into everyday behaviour.

Sex education

Human relationships are complex; we learn to build relationships or to simply co-exist with one another, to deal with conflict, manage problems or end toxic relationships. Things become more complicated when sex is brought into the equation. One thing is for certain: it is important that sex education is inclusive, which can be extremely challenging. In their book *Values in Sex Education*, Mark Halstead and Michael Reiss (2003) state, 'When it comes to opinions about sex, people all too often inhabit different worlds, speak different languages, hold incompatible and widely divergent views. The situation is further complicated by differences compounded by gender, social class, culture and other factors, and by the existence of numerous pressure groups each with a different agenda, and often each talking at cross-purposes with the others, vying for influence in sex education policy.' There is a diversity of 'sexual' values that are accepted by different members of society, including teachers themselves, who could unconsciously transmit their own values and beliefs. This is one of the reasons why it is crucial to provide training to those who will be involved in the delivery of lessons. If staff lack confidence, knowledge or skills, they will not be able to deliver sensitive content to the class.

Healthy sexual relationships

Part of learning about how to become a healthier partner is learning to have healthy sexual relationships. In order to have healthy sexual relationships, we need to have knowledge of human bodies (including puberty and reproductive organs) and how to protect our bodies during intercourse (with contraception). This applies to all pupils – trans, homosexual, bisexual, pansexual and heterosexual – as it is our responsibility to keep all of our young people safe.

In their book *Great Relationships and Sex Education*, Alice Hoyle and Ester McGeeney (2020) provide many activities that could be used with smaller or larger groups of pupils. Making a PSHE classroom a safe place should be our ongoing priority: having a learning agreement, approaching contributions in a non-judgmental way, allowing time for reflection and having a debrief at the end of the lesson are some of the strategies we could use to achieve this goal. In order to ensure consistency in delivery, it is important to provide as much support to staff as possible in terms of training, observations, working groups, etc. In the meantime, if you have doubts about RSE delivery, it might be worth considering inviting outside agencies, for example charities, who possess knowledge and skills to deliver the sessions. One of the best sessions I have observed was delivered by an NHS outreach support worker who visited the school as part of the C-Card training programme.

Before pupils become sexually active, it is also important to introduce the topic of consent, including assumptions relating to consent, the right to withdraw consent and the capacity to consent (for example, how alcohol or drug use can impede our decision-making). Brook (www.brook.org.uk) has many resources rooted in research to educate staff and enable them to teach this sensitive topic. One of my favourite activities is The Consent Continuum developed by the researcher Elsie Whittington. She shows that 'yes' and 'no' cannot always be used to categorise sexual experiences, and introduces categories like 'rape', 'non-consensual sex', 'passive consent' and 'active consent' to demonstrate the complexities and grey areas associated with the term 'consent'.

An inclusive RSE curriculum is essential to protect all pupils, in particular those who are LGBTQ+. According to the website Your Sexual Health Matters, 'Gay and bisexual men, and men who have sex with men (MSM), are more likely to encounter sexually transmitted infections (STIs).' Furthermore, research conducted by The Human Rights Campaign showed that 'LGBTQ youth have a limited number of trusted adults they feel comfortable talking with about sexual health, so they frequently seek information online or from peers. Much of the sexual health information online is neither age-appropriate nor medically accurate, and peers may be misinformed.' It is important that we design an inclusive curriculum where young people should be able to see themselves reflected in the curriculum. It could be useful to co-produce resources with young people as this would increase inclusivity and relevance – RSE learning could well take place outside of the school in more informal ways. This way we narrow the gap between their experiences and the school curriculum: we won't know what knowledge they already have if we don't ask, so baseline assessments are always helpful. It is also important that we, as a school, create an environment where our pupils can be themselves and be accepted for who they are, so that they develop trust and a sense of belonging, which is essential for their wellbeing. However, once again, it is only possible if the school culture is one of inclusion, diversity, respect and empathy.

Reflections

1. What values do you reinforce through your RSE provision?

_____

_____

_____

_____

_____

2. Do your staff have knowledge and understanding of the relationships part of the RSE curriculum?

_____

_____

_____

_____

_____

3. How is sex education delivered in your setting? Is it inclusive?

_____

_____

_____

_____

_____

4. What are you already doing in terms of RSE to support each of the wellbeing areas?

Physical and mental health	Emotional health	Social health	Spiritual health

5. What else can be done to enhance RSE provision?

_____

_____

_____

6. Can other departments contribute to the provision to ensure a whole-school approach?

_____

_____

_____

9 Evaluating impact: how to measure wellbeing

Overview

This chapter will:

- discuss the challenges of measuring wellbeing and therefore determining the impact of proactive pastoral care
- offer practical methods for measuring pupil wellbeing and tracking mental health.

As you begin to implement proactive pastoral care in your school, it is important that you measure, monitor and evaluate the impact of what you are doing with your pupils. Ensuring and enhancing the wellbeing of pupils is the key objective of pastoral care; however, one of the questions I get asked a lot is: 'How do we measure wellbeing?' As we have seen, there exists a range of definitions of wellbeing, depending on wellbeing theories. It comes as no surprise therefore that there is little agreement in the research literature on how best to measure wellbeing. As Taylor (2015) suggests, 'the prospects of consensus seem remote, since there are a number of rival theories, and no obvious means of resolving the debate between them.'

The challenges of measuring wellbeing

The research highlights a number of further difficulties when measuring wellbeing:

1. It is not possible to assess wellbeing as a concept; only a particular area of wellbeing can be measured at once.
2. Wellbeing is a subjective matter.
3. The meaning of wellbeing can depend on cultural differences.
4. A tick-box approach to measuring wellbeing can be dangerous.

Let's look at each in turn.

1. It is not possible to assess wellbeing as a concept

As Pollard and Lee (2003) state, 'Researchers often report that they are measuring a child's well-being when in fact they are assessing a single domain or indicator of well-being, not recognizing they are merely assessing an aspect of well-being.' Alexandrova (2017) argues that wellbeing can be measured, but we must 'predicate well-being of kinds of people in specific circumstances'. In other words, similarly to Pollard and Lee, the researcher believes that measuring overall individual wellbeing is problematic but is optimistic about measuring certain specific aspects of wellbeing, such as happiness, mental health and meaningful work.

2. A subjective matter

It is very difficult to compare the wellbeing of two or more individuals because wellbeing is such a subjective experience. When someone is invited to evaluate their own wellbeing, their answer will depend on 'the quality of their own experience, their feeling of being happy and contented, their sense of well-being'. In this context, we can only ascertain someone's levels of wellbeing through their behaviour or how they report on their wellbeing verbally (Campbell, quoted in Brümmer and Sarot, 1996). Dolan et al. (2008) also claim that 'subjective well-being (SWB) is often used by psychologists as an umbrella term for how we think and feel about our lives.' The term can incorporate many different evaluations like joy, feeling and emotions, or fulfilment in personal or professional life. We ourselves make an evaluation of our lives: what is going well according to the criteria that I myself chose?

3. Cultural differences

It is also important to bear in mind that the meaning of wellbeing and other related terms can be dependent on cultural background. You will recall the various definitions of wellbeing from Chapters 2 and 3. As Carlquist et al. (2017) state, 'great care must be taken when drawing cross-cultural conclusions' because 'in spite of pervasive globalization, a variety of cultural norms and traditions still inform individual and social behaviors'. It's important to remember this when attempting to measure wellbeing among diverse communities of staff and pupils from different cultural backgrounds.

4. The dangers of a tick-box approach

Alexandrova (2017) questions 'whether the science of well-being is a morally and politically justified pursuit. This field is riding a wave of popularity and excitement for reasons that are not altogether uplifting.' She explores the idea that wellbeing is 'propped up' by consumerism and capitalism, with a lucrative industry and work culture where workers must be happy in their jobs no matter what and consumers must be happy but also just unhappy enough to keep consuming. Bevan and Hood (2006) also make a valid point: 'benchmarking in healthcare and education provides a wealth of depressing examples for how the pursuit of targets in the guise of accountability introduces perverse incentives and destroys trust and quality for all involved.' As professionals, we must be aware of the dangers that come with measuring wellbeing. Leaders must ensure that the data is used not for a tick-box exercise or for promoting accountability and setting some sort of unachievable wellbeing targets, but for the purpose of genuinely enhancing pastoral provision and providing relevant training and interventions.

So, what can be done?

Despite all these difficulties, a number of studies around measuring subjective wellbeing have been published and this is a field that is expanding at the current time. Diener et al. (2008) calculate that 'There are now about 2,000 publications per year on topics generally related to the subject of subjective well-being, and many more when ill-being is included.'

In this section, I am going to look first at some early studies that attempted to measure wellbeing and then at some more contemporary groups and surveys that have sought to do the same over recent years. The purpose of providing this research is once again to highlight the complex nature of wellbeing, give it back the status and the meaning that have been lost due to poor understanding and implementation of wellbeing within our work communities, and seek out approaches to measure and evaluate it.

Early attempts to measure wellbeing

So, if we turn to history, we find that the researcher J. C. Flügel was attempting to measure and evaluate wellbeing as early as 1925. He asked people to record emotional events and their emotional reactions. As Diener et al. (2008) say, 'Flügel's work was the forerunner of modern experience sampling approaches to measuring subjective well-being online as people go about their everyday lives.' Another influential early study of happiness was Goodwin Watson's (1930) 'Happiness among adult students of education'. Watson considered the influence of many factors on happiness in adult students, including family size, age, IQ and school grades, but found that these did not predict happiness among his subjects. Instead, he concluded that sex and marriage were the central factors related to happiness.

A further study is described by Randolph C. Sailer (1931), who worked with Goodwin Watson at Columbia University. Sailer conducted his own test to measure individual happiness among male students aged 17 to 35. He found a correlation between happiness, good health and strong faith. He also linked what he called 'an even temper' with happiness, explaining that students who experienced constant and consistent emotions were happier than those who experienced severe mood swings.

Contemporary research

According to Diener et al. (2008), between 1961 and 2005 the number of publications per year pertaining to life-satisfaction and happiness increased from merely a handful to about 300 for each topic. So, what are these more contemporary studies, what are they attempting to measure and what can we learn from them? We will consider the following studies in this section:

Researcher or group	Study
Government of Bhutan	Gross National Happiness Index
The World Values Survey Association	World Values Survey, tracking values and beliefs
The University of Minnesota and Southern Methodist University	Positive and Negative Affect Schedule (PANAS)
The Economic and Social Research Council	British Household Panel Study and Understanding Society UK Household Longitudinal Study

Researcher or group	Study
The European Social Survey	European Social Survey, measuring happiness and life satisfaction
Gallup	Gallup World Poll, with thriving, struggling and suffering indexes
Sonja Lyubomirsky	Subjective Happiness Scale
Christopher Peterson and Martin Seligman	VIA Inventory of Strengths (VIA-IS)
Michael Argyle and Peter Hills, Oxford Brookes University	Oxford Happiness Questionnaire
Joseph Stiglitz, Amartya Sen and Jean-Paul Fitoussi	Report of the Commission on the Measurement of Economic Performance and Social Progress
OECD	Guidelines on Measuring Subjective Well-being

Gross National Happiness Index

Date: 1972 to present

Factors measured: 33 indicators categorised under nine domains: psychological wellbeing, health, education, use of time, cultural diversity and resilience, good governance, community vitality, ecological diversity and resilience, and living standards

Detail: In 1972, the country of Bhutan designed the Gross National Happiness (GNH) Index, a single-number index developed from 33 indicators in the nine domains listed above. The Index uses a robust methodology known as the Alkire-Foster method. The Alkire-Foster method was developed by Sabina Alkire and James Foster and became a flexible technique for measuring poverty or wellbeing. It can incorporate different dimensions and indicators to create measures adapted to specific contexts, and has been adapted by several countries to develop their national measures.

World Values Survey

Date: 1981 to present

Factors measured: values, beliefs, life evaluation, overall happiness, mood and psychological wellbeing

Detail: In 1981, The World Values Survey was launched to track people's values and beliefs, how they change over time, and what social and political impact they have. Many social scientists have conducted surveys in various countries, although the sampling has varied over time. It contains measures of life evaluation and overall happiness, as well as more focused measures of experienced mood and aspects of psychological wellbeing in recent surveys. The seventh wave of the World Values Survey is taking place as I write (between 2017 and 2020) and is monitoring a variety of factors, including cultural values, attitudes and beliefs towards gender, family, and religion; attitudes and experience of poverty; education, health, and security; and social tolerance and trust.

Positive and Negative Affect Schedule

Date: 1988 to present

Factors measured: positive and negative emotions

Detail: The Positive and Negative Affect Schedule (PANAS) was developed in 1988 by researchers from the University of Minnesota and Southern Methodist University. PANAS is a self-report questionnaire that consists of two mood scales, one that measures positive affect (meaning emotions) and another that measures negative affect. The mood scales each include ten terms used to describe emotions – one including positive terms and the other negative terms – and respondents indicate to what extent they are experiencing each emotion. It can show relations between positive and negative affect with personality traits.

British Household Panel Study and Understanding Society UK Household Longitudinal Study

Date: 1991 to present

Factors measured: experiences of life in the UK, including a range of social, economic and behavioural factors

Detail: The British Household Panel Study was launched in 1991 and was later integrated into the Understanding Society UK Household Longitudinal Study, funded by the Economic and Social Research Council and a consortium of government departments. There is a special questionnaire for children aged ten to 15 and an adult survey for those aged 16 and over. As the data is collected annually and is so wide-ranging, there is an opportunity to investigate short-term and long-term changes in people's lives and thus allow researchers to analyse a wealth of information, including responses to subjective wellbeing questions.

European Social Survey

Date: 2002 to present

Factors measured: subjective wellbeing: happiness and life satisfaction

Detail: This survey collects a rich dataset on wellbeing across European countries every two years. There is a core questionnaire that includes summary measures of subjective wellbeing, plus thematic 'rotating modules' vary each time to collect more in-depth data on different aspects of wellbeing. The ESS core questionnaire includes the two most common measures of subjective wellbeing: happiness and life satisfaction. While happiness is usually conceptualised in terms of people's emotional responses and measures their current feelings, life satisfaction is conceptualised in terms of their cognitive or evaluative responses and measures how people evaluate their life as a whole (Clark and Senik, 2011).

Gallup World Poll

Date: 2005 to present

Factors measured: life satisfaction and daily wellbeing

Detail: The Gallup World Poll started in 2005 and Gallup CEO Jim Clifton claimed that 'it will forever change how world leaders lead'. In the first wave taking place between 2005 and 2009, the poll consisted of face-to-face and telephone interviews with approximately 1,000 adults, aged 15 and older, from 155 different countries. The poll measures respondents' perceptions of where they stand now and how they think about their future. It uses the Cantril Self-Anchoring Striving Scale to measure life satisfaction, asking respondents to rate their present and future lives on a scale from 0 to 10, where 0 indicates the worst possible life and 10 the best possible life. Individuals are then classified according to their responses. Those who rate their current lives as 7 or higher and their future as 8 or higher are considered to be 'thriving'. Individuals who report their current *and* future lives as 4 or lower are considered to be 'suffering'. All other respondents are considered to be 'struggling'.

The poll also measures daily wellbeing averages (from 0 to 10) by asking questions around daily experiences, including feeling well-rested, being treated with respect, smiling and laughter, learning and interest, enjoyment, physical pain, worry, sadness, stress and anger.

Subjective Happiness Scale

Date: 1999 to present

Factors measured: subjective happiness

Detail: The Subjective Happiness Scale was developed in 1999 by Sonja Lyubomirsky. It had 13 original items to reflect an individual's overall subjective happiness. However, six items were dropped because they were found to be too similar in meaning, and an additional three items were dropped when an analysis demonstrated that they did not load onto a single factor. The survey now has four questions, two of which are designed in a way that asks respondents to characterise themselves using both absolute ratings and ratings relative to peers, whereas the other two items offer brief descriptions of happy and unhappy individuals and ask respondents the extent to which each characterisation describes them.

VIA Inventory of Strengths

Date: 2000 to present

Factors measured: character strengths

Detail: In 2000, Christopher Peterson and Martin Seligman piloted the VIA Inventory of Strengths (VIA-IS), formerly known as the 'Values in Action Inventory'. This is a psychological assessment measure that is designed to identify an individual's profile of character strengths. Positive psychology researchers developed a 240-item self-report questionnaire intended for use with adults. The measure uses a five-point scale to measure the degree to which respondents endorse items reflecting the 24 strengths of character that comprise the VIA Classification. A shorter version of the questionnaire and descriptions of the 24 strengths are available on their website at www.viacharacter.org.

Oxford Happiness Questionnaire

Date: 2002 to present

Factors measured: happiness

Detail: In 2002, the Oxford Happiness Questionnaire (OHQ) was developed by Michael Argyle and Peter Hills of Oxford Brookes University, and originally published in the *Journal of Personality and Individual Differences*. It lists 29 statements about happiness, and respondents rate how much they agree or disagree with each on a scale of 1 to 6, where 1 is strongly disagree and 6 is strongly agree. The questionnaire has been described as 'compact, easy to administer and allows endorsements over an extended range'.

Report of the Commission on the Measurement of Economic Performance and Social Progress

Date: 2009

Factors measured: subjective wellbeing, including cognitive evaluations of a person's life, positive emotions and negative emotions

Detail: This isn't a survey in itself but a report that provides some useful guidelines for how national statistic agencies could incorporate questions on subjective wellbeing. In 2009, the Report of the Commission on the Measurement of Economic Performance and Social Progress noted that 'Recent research has shown that it is possible to collect meaningful and reliable data on subjective wellbeing.' They define subjective wellbeing in terms of three different aspects: cognitive evaluations of one's life, positive emotions (such as joy and pride) and negative emotions (such as pain, anger and worry). The report admitted that many different factors affecting these aspects of subjective wellbeing have different determinants, but that one thing was clear: all factors go well beyond income and material conditions. The advice the report gave was for each of these three aspects of subjective wellbeing to be measured separately to give a clearer understanding of quality of life and its determinants. They suggested that national statistical agencies should add questions on subjective wellbeing to their existing surveys to capture 'people's life evaluations, hedonic experiences and life priorities'.

OECD Guidelines on Measuring Subjective Well-being

Date: 2013

Factors measured: subjective wellbeing, including life evaluation, feelings or emotional states and eudaimonia (a sense of purpose or good psychological functioning)

Detail: Again, this is a set of guidelines for measuring wellbeing, rather than a survey or questionnaire in itself. The Organization for Economic Cooperation and Development (OECD) issued guidelines on measuring subjective wellbeing in 2013. The guidelines were produced under the Better Life Initiative launched by the organisation in 2011 with the aim of measuring 11 domains of wellbeing, particularly people's thoughts and experiences of life, as well as 'to contribute to a greater consistency in measurement of subjective well-being in official statistics' (OECD, 2013). For the purpose of these guidelines, wellbeing is defined as 'Good mental states, including all of the various evaluations, positive and negative, that people make of their lives and the affective reactions of people to their experiences'. The OECD identified three elements in their definition:

- **Life evaluation:** a reflective assessment on life or a specific aspect of it
- **Affect:** feelings or emotional states, typically measured with reference to a particular point in time
- **Eudaimonia:** meaning and purpose in life, or good general psychological functioning.

The influence of positive psychology on measuring wellbeing

The positive psychology movement focused on researching the strengths and virtues that contribute to human flourishing. Positive psychology accepts that certain character traits are more conducive to subjective wellbeing than others, but what exactly are those traits and how do they promote wellbeing? Researchers also ask themselves whether it is worth tracking certain virtues, such as optimism, that help to support leading a good life. This is supported by the transpersonal movement, which proposes 'that the study of positives states and qualities of functioning should be incorporated into our efforts at constructing a more complete and holistic understanding of the individual. Consequently, health is seen not merely as the absence of pathology but instead as the presence of growth-orientedness and a movement toward well-being and self-realization'. (Elmer et al., 2003) If we place this philosophy at the heart of measuring wellbeing in schools, it is clear that we should be evaluating the strengths and abilities of young people in order to discover what will enable them to grow and thrive.

*

Looking at the history of approaches to measuring wellbeing reveals that, although they differ considerably, one thing they have in common is that they are designed to measure a certain area of wellbeing. Therefore, the title 'wellbeing assessment', which is used by many professionals in education, seems to be quite confusing or even misleading, as it does not specify what area of wellbeing is being assessed. When we are measuring wellbeing and evaluating the progress made by pastoral care, we must be as specific as possible: what area are we focusing on? Why? How are we going to assess this area? What type of data do we need to collect? Who needs to be involved in data collection? Why?

Measuring child wellbeing

Measuring adult and child wellbeing differs significantly for a variety of reasons: for one, adults could have more experience and emotional wisdom and express their feelings with greater clarity than children. Measuring pupil wellbeing has attracted a lot of attention nationally; many politicians, policymakers, teachers, wellbeing consultants, psychologists and charities have been taking part in the debate. United Children's Fund report on child wellbeing in wealthy countries (UNICEF, 2013), ranking the UK 16th out of 29 developed countries. The report did at least show a strong improvement in this country's rankings: the UK has moved from bottom place (21st out of 21 countries) in 2000/1 to a mid-table position. The report also highlights some problem areas: a high percentage of young people (83 per cent) found it easier to talk to mothers compared to 68 per cent of children who found it easier to talk to fathers. Only 63 per cent of UK children found classmates kind and helpful. Nonetheless, a number of researchers have confirmed that there has been some improvement in the area of wellbeing. According to Rees and Main (2016), 'happiness with schoolwork appears to have increased from 2009/10–2012/13.'

Despite stated improvements, current statistics are still worrying. The Children's Society (2020) report recently promoted by the media claims that more than a fifth of 14-year-old girls in the UK self-harm (Therrien, 2018). According to the Mental Health Foundation (2018), ten per cent of children and young people (aged five to 16 years) have a clinically diagnosable mental health problem. Seventy per cent of children and adolescents who experience mental health problems have not had appropriate interventions at a sufficiently early age. Fifty per cent of mental health problems are established by the age of 14. In 2013 there were 6,233 suicides recorded in the UK for people aged 15 and older (78 per cent were male and 22 per cent were female). As a teacher and a parent, I have heard many worrying personal stories, and the data quoted by some major newspapers seems to confirm them. In 2016 the *Independent* claimed that 'the number of children in the UK prescribed anti-depressants increased by more than 50 per cent between 2005 and 2012' (Stubbs, 2016). In their 2017 article published in the *Journal of Affective Disorders*, Sarginson et al. (2017) state that 'rates of antidepressant prescribing to children aged 3–17 doubled between 2006 and 2015 in the UK.'

With this bleak picture in mind, schools have started to look for ways to tackle the area of wellbeing. Traditionally, safeguarding referred to protecting pupils from abuse and neglect. Safeguarding in Schools outlines the following safeguarding responsibilities:

1. 'protecting children from maltreatment;

2. preventing impairment of children's health or development;

3. ensuring that children grow up in circumstances consistent with the provision of safe and effective care;

4. and taking action to enable all children to have the best outcomes.'

As we can see, the word 'wellbeing' is not mentioned once and many would use the terms 'safeguarding' and 'child protection' interchangeably despite the fact that they mean different things: child protection refers to children who are at a significant risk of harm. For many schools, the concept of wellbeing is a new concept, and with minimum guidance and lack of training, education communities are left to work out ways for themselves on how to approach this important pastoral area. As a result, we can observe a variety of approaches and a variety of companies using the term 'wellbeing' in their promotional materials to offer quick-fix solutions. But quick fixes are neither proactive nor long-term solutions. We must be looking to proactive pastoral provision and evaluating it closely to ensure that it can have a genuine impact on wellbeing in the long term.

How to evaluate impact by measuring wellbeing

As we have seen, there are many issues to take into account before embarking on the journey of measuring wellbeing. The reason why I use the word 'journey' is because measuring wellbeing is a fluid process. Wellbeing at the start of the year might measure completely differently compared to the end of the year, for example. Wellbeing in Year 6 could be very different to wellbeing in Year 7 due to a number of changes that would have taken place.

So, how do we translate all that wellbeing research into action? Here are two main takeaways:

1. Try using digital tools to measure wellbeing.

2. Design a bespoke questionnaire suitable for measuring wellbeing in your own school community.

I will now look at each in a little more detail.

Using digital tools

There are a number of platforms that might offer useful tools to help you measure your pupils' wellbeing. Once again, use critical thinking when making decisions about which tool to use, asking yourself:

- What exactly is being measured?
- Is it appropriate for our school community?
- What data would we be receiving?
- Would it help us to move forward? How?

Here is a list of some useful platforms to get you started:

- Motivational Map
- Bounce Together

- Voxpop
- AS tracker
- CORC
- Voice of the Student
- BETLS
- Boxall
- Leuven Scales
- PASS survey
- Thrive Approach
- Edukit.

I will consider the ones that have been frequently mentioned to me in more detail below.

Bounce Together

According to their website, www.bouncetogether.co.uk, Bounce Together is 'a game-changing digital platform for measuring and continually monitoring the wellbeing, behaviours, health, perceptions and attitudes of your school's pupils and staff'. Bounce software has been produced by a team with decades of experience working in software development and education. They have adopted a 'Five Ways of Well-being' concept from the New Economics Foundation, encompassing:

1. connect
2. be active
3. take notice
4. keep learning
5. give.

But how were these Five Ways identified? Between July 2006 and October 2008, the government's Chief Scientific Adviser and Head of the Government Office for Science, Sir David King, commissioned a project titled 'Mental capital and wellbeing: Making the most of ourselves in the 21st century project'. The project draws upon the advice of over 400 leading experts and stakeholders from countries across the world, specialising in a whole range of disciplines from economics to social sciences and ethics, neuroscience, psychology and psychiatry. Towards the end of the project, the New Economics Foundation was commissioned to develop an evidence-based set of daily activities that support people's wellbeing; as a result, the Five Ways listed above were identified.

These five ways have been used extensively by many charities and wellbeing organisations: Mind, NHS and the Mental Health Foundation, just to name a few. Bounce Together is not an exception to the rule. Although the Five Ways is a well-researched concept, a product of collaboration involving many experts from different fields, it is the implementation of the concept that needs to be looked at more closely. Bounce Together offers you two options:

1. **Pre-loaded content:** There is a library of validated questionnaires that you can choose from, covering behaviour, safety, mindset, resilience, mental health, wellbeing, empathy and more.

2. **Create your own:** A questionnaire-builder enables you to create your own questions with a variety of question types.

It is hard to evaluate the questionnaires without seeing them, and I would be interested to know what questions have been included, how they have been chosen, what language is used and whether it is tailored to specific year groups.

AS Tracking

AS Tracking would cost a secondary school of 700 to 800 pupils around £15,000 per year. According to the website (https://steer.global/en/products/as-tracking), 'AS Tracking, short for *Affective*

Social Tracking, is a breakthrough adolescent mental health tracking tool that enables schools to identify pupils' hidden risks early.' They claim there is evidence that shows AS Tracking improves whole-school and individual pupil wellbeing 'by equipping teachers with in-school, targeted action plans to reduce pupil mental health and wellbeing risks'.

The website also states that AS Tracking works by tracking the 'steering biases' that are developing in the mind of a student. Tracking steering biases is pioneering technology developed by 20 years of research involving thousands of students. Steering biases influence the health of the social and emotional relationships that a student forms, their developing mental health and their social competencies. As with any type of tracking, it is important to question the reliability of the data provided for your specific context and remain mindful of not stereotyping pupils and making assumptions when using tools such as this.

Warwick-Edinburgh Mental Well-being Scale

The Warwick-Edinburgh Mental Well-being Scale (WEMWBS) was developed in 2007 by a panel of experts at several UK universities, including Warwick, Edinburgh, Anglia Ruskin, Queen Mary University of London and Bristol, and representatives of NHS Health Scotland and the Centre for Psychiatry at Barts and the London. The website states that 'WEMWBS represents mental wellbeing as:

- Both feeling good and functioning well. The scales therefore cover:
  - eudemonic and hedonic wellbeing (as talked about in the ancient philosophical context)
  - psychological functioning and subjective wellbeing (as talked about in current psychology and social science research).'

According to the user guide, 'past research and practice surrounding mental health and wellbeing have focused on mental health problems and on prevention of developing a mental disorder (mental health problem), rather than on mental wellbeing. However, not much data have been gathered at larger population levels on levels of mental wellbeing or trends over time. Collecting before and after project data can tell us a lot about what strategies work best and what helps people improve and sustain mental wellbeing.'

There are two versions of the questionnaire: the 14-item and the seven-item version. The 14-item version is the original, providing a fuller picture of mental wellbeing using feeling and functioning items. It can be used when you need a full picture of mental wellbeing. The seven-item version is more concise, meaning that it can save you time, plus it 'has better scaling properties which means that the measurements of differences in scores may be more precise'.

Boxall Profile

An older pupil wellbeing measurement worth mentioning is the Boxall Profile, which 'was developed as part of the nurture group movement'. This originated in Hackney in 1969, and was a 'response of Marjorie Boxall, an educational psychologist, to the high levels of distress in primary schools at a time of great social upheaval and teacher shortage'. The Boxall Profile assesses social, emotional and behavioural development of children and young people. There are two tests available – one for younger children and one for older children – and the test is set automatically online based on the date of birth entered by a pupil. On completion, 'the scores of each individual student are compared to the standardised emotional literacy scores of "competently functioning" children of a similar age group. Individualised, achievable targets for social and emotional aptitudes are then set for the student which are reviewed and re-assessed periodically.'

According to Philpot and Tomlinson (2008), the Boxall Profile 'was originally devised as a structured observational tool to assist teachers to plan a focused intervention in the classroom' and replaced Dockar-Drysdale's needs assessment from 1970. In 1997, it was endorsed by the then Department for Education and Employment, who said it was useful 'in assisting inclusiveness, enhancing teachers' skills in managing children with emotional and behavioural difficulties, and in developing strategies that lead to effective early interventions'.

Mood and Feelings Questionnaire

The Mood and Feelings Questionnaire (MFQ) was developed by Adrian Angold and Elizabeth J. Costello in 1987 and focuses on measuring childhood and adolescent depression. The authors focused on 30 symptoms 'reflecting current clinical and taxonomic thinking about childhood depression, which tapped affective, cognitive, vegetative and suicidal aspects of depression'. They selected only those symptoms that are central to the concept of depression, rather than related symptoms such as enuresis, wandering behaviour and school phobia. They attempted to make the questionnaire as simple as possible, so each item consists of a single sentence to which the subject can respond 'Not true', 'Sometimes' or 'True'. Child and parent versions of the questionnaire are available free online at https://devepi.duhs.duke.edu/measures/the-mood-and-feelings-questionnaire-mfq and have been translated into a number of languages.

*

As we have seen, there are a number of tools that schools could use to assess wellbeing. It is important that leaders, as decision-makers, pause, take a step back and use their knowledge of wellbeing and their community to make a decision that would benefit their young people and enhance pastoral provision.

Bespoke wellbeing questionnaire

You are the expert in your community and you will know its make-up in terms of staff and pupil backgrounds, the problems that you need to address, and your key priorities. You can use this knowledge to come up with your own short questionnaires to investigate certain problems relating to one of the wellbeing areas. I am not suggesting that you should aim to design a scientific questionnaire – more of a quick poll to gain an understanding of what you are dealing with, and to give you an indication of where progress is being made and where further attention is required. Remember that these evaluations should be specific and should aim to measure one particular area of wellbeing.

Here are some questions to start the thinking process:

- What area of wellbeing do we need to measure?
- Is there a specific issue that needs investigating further?
- Is this an issue for all year groups or just a particular year group?
- Is this an issue for boys or girls?
- What type of data needs to be collected to help us solve the issue?
- What could stop us from collecting the data?
- How could we overcome the obstacles?
- Do we need to involve the extended pastoral community?

Every single community is unique, and it would be wrong for someone without the knowledge of the context to choose a particular way of measuring wellbeing for you: it is important that you choose something that will work for you as a community and something that would bring positive sustainable changes that would enhance your pastoral provision.

Reflections

1. Do you think it's important to measure staff wellbeing and pupil wellbeing?

_____

_____

2. Can the four wellbeing areas be measured? What are you already doing to analyse wellbeing in each of these areas? What more could you do?

Physical and mental health	Emotional health	Social health	Spiritual health

3. What would be appropriate for your community: a ready-made questionnaire, an in-house-produced questionnaire or a combination of both? Why?

_____

_____

_____

4. How could the outcomes of these questionnaires contribute towards the development of your pastoral provision?

_____

_____

_____

Conclusion: how proactive is your pastoral care?

Now that we are at the end of the book, I would like to turn to the most important question: how do we know how proactive our school structures are? In answer to this question, I am going to present sample whole-school self-evaluation questions that could serve as a baseline assessment or become part of short-, medium- or long-term audits.

All the questions refer to different areas that have been discussed in the chapters of this book. They can be used together as part of a larger audit or separately to enable you to focus on a particular area. You can change or amend the questions to suit your particular context, but I believe they could provide a good starting point when evaluating your pastoral care.

Whole school

- What are the school values?
  (They should underpin your direction and your actions as a school community.)

- Why were they chosen?
  (This question helps you to reflect and reconnect to your 'why'.)

- How do we know that they are understood by the school community: staff (including support staff), pupils, governors and parents?
  (The answers will show whether the values are truly embedded.)

- How do values underpin your policies?
  (One of the first things I did when I took on responsibility for e-safety was to rewrite our acceptable use policy (AUP) and base it on values.)

- Are there opportunities for pupils to put values into action?
  (The answers will show if the values are practised, not only spoken about.)

Pastoral structure

- Do you have a key member of staff who is responsible for the wellbeing of pupils?
  (Usually the responsibility is diluted among various members of pastoral staff. Although every single member of staff should be responsible for the wellbeing of the pupils they teach or have in their tutor group, there should be someone with overall responsibility who has a bigger picture and is empowered to think strategically.)

- Do you have a key member of staff who is responsible for the wellbeing of staff?
  (Although headteachers have overall responsibility for their staff wellbeing, very often direct responsibility is allocated to someone who is in charge of teaching and learning and staff CPD, or who acts as deputy head pastoral. As these members of staff already have a lot on their plate, they do not always have the capacity to focus on staff wellbeing and it can be put on the back burner. As a result, we can have members of staff without the correct wellbeing knowledge or skills acting as role models for our young people.)

- Are these key members of staff senior leaders?
  (In order to make a difference, it's important that these members of staff have senior status and actively contribute to the school development plan.)

- Is the member of staff responsible for pupil wellbeing also responsible for safeguarding?

(It would be more beneficial to separate safeguarding and proactive pastoral care to ensure that the person in charge of the latter has the time and head space to think strategically rather than operationally.)

- How many of your SLT are pastoral leaders?
  (Is there a balance? Often the composition of SLT clearly demonstrates a school's priorities.)
- Who are the members of your pastoral team and are they working well as a team?
  (It is important that the pastoral team meets regularly and all members with safeguarding and proactive care responsibility are working towards the same vision in a collaborative and supportive way.)

Pastoral curriculum

- How is pastoral curriculum embedded in your context?
  (Once again, this could be an indication of how valued pastoral care is by governors and SLT.)
- Is your community (governors and parents) aware of what is being covered and do they have an opportunity to contribute to planning and delivery?
- Is the pastoral curriculum valued by staff? How do you know?
  (If staff value the pastoral curriculum, this will be passed on to the pupils, as the way they prepare and deliver lessons will be different.)
- Is the pastoral curriculum valued by pupils? How do you know?
  (If it's not, what can you do to raise the status of the pastoral curriculum?)
- Do you know if or how much academic departments contribute to the pastoral curriculum?
  (For example, I have done a whole-school audit of how much other departments contribute to the delivery of RSE.)

Co-curriculum

- Is there a member of staff responsible for the co-curricular life of the school?
  (It might be as part of another responsibility.)

- What activities are offered and how do they contribute to character development outside the classroom?

- Do staff actively engage with the co-curricular life of school?
  (The reason for this question is to explore further the workload of staff and their capacity to offer co-curricular opportunities whether whole-school or relating to their particular subject area.)

- Do pupils value and take advantage of co-curricular opportunities on offer?

- Is the co-curriculum agenda discussed as part of school meetings?
  (Working with other key pastoral and academic staff members ensures that the co-curriculum truly becomes an extension of the school curriculum, both pastoral and academic.)

Community involvement

- Are there opportunities for parents to contribute to decision-making relating to pastoral care and wellbeing?
  (This could include focus groups or forums for parents.)

- Have the parents been involved in organising pastoral events?
  (Pastoral events that are organised by parents for parents can attract more attendees.)

- How aware are parents of what is being delivered within the pastoral curriculum?
  (It is important that parents are aware and they are given an opportunity to reinforce learning at home.)

- How and how often is pastoral training delivered to parents?
  (This could include formal and informal opportunities.)

This is not an exclusive list of questions, but it is a good starting point. More questions could be added to look specifically at student support and the roles of heads of year, pastoral managers, tutors, and so on. You can develop the questions to suit your context and refer back to the chapters in this book for further support, guidance and ideas.

I wish you every success on your pastoral journey. Don't forget to keep an eye on support materials that can be found online at www.proactivepastoralcare.co.uk.

References

Alexandrova, A. (2017), *A Philosophy for the Science of Well-Being.* Oxford: Oxford University Press.

Arthur, J., Kristjánsson, K., Walker, D., Sanderse, W. and Jones, C. (2015), 'Character education in UK schools: Research report'. Birmingham: Jubilee Centre for Character and Virtues.

Averill, J. R. (1980), 'A constructivist view of emotion', in: R. Plutchik and H. Kellerman (Eds.), *Emotion: Theory, research, and experience. Volume 1: Theories of emotion.* New York, NY: Academic Press.

Barry, H. (2018), *Emotional Resilience.* London: Orion Spring.

Barry, M. M., Clarke, A. M. and Dowling, K. (2017), 'Promoting social and emotional well-being in schools', *Health Education,* 117, (5), 434–451.

Beedie, C., Terry, P. and Lane, A. (2005), 'Distinctions between emotion and mood', *Cognition and Emotion,* 19, (6), 847–878.

Beland, L.-P. (2015), 'Ill communication: technology, distraction and student performance', *Labour Economics,* 41, 61–76.

Bell, L. and Maher, P. (1986), *Leading a Pastoral Team.* Oxford: Blackwell.

Benson, P. L., Roehlkepartain, E. C. and Rude, S. P. (2003), 'Spiritual development in childhood and adolescence: Toward a field of inquiry', *Applied Developmental Science,* 7, (3), 205–213.

Berkowitz, M. W. (1997), 'The complete moral person: Anatomy and formation', in: J. M. DuBois (Ed.), *Moral Issues in Psychology: Personalist contributions to selected problems.* Lanham, MD: University Press of America.

Berkowitz, M. W. and Bier, M. C. (2007), 'What works in character education', *Journal of Research in Character Education,* 5, (1), 29–48.

Best, R. (2014), 'Forty years of *Pastoral Care*: an appraisal of Michael Marland's seminal book and its significance for pastoral care in schools', *Pastoral Care in Education,* 32, (3), 173–185.

Bevan, G. and Hood, C. (2006), 'What's measured is what matters: targets and gaming in the English Public Health care system', *Public Administration,* 84, (3), 517–538.

Birdwell, J., Scott, R. and Reynolds, L. (2015), 'Character nation: A Demos report with the Jubilee Centre for Character and Virtues'. London: Demos.

Blakemore, S. J. (2018), *Inventing Ourselves: The secret life of the teenage brain.* London: Transworld.

Bowater, D. (2012), 'Internet addiction affects the brain "like a drink or drug problem"', *Telegraph*, www.telegraph.co.uk/technology/internet/9009125/Internet-addiction-affects-the-brain-like-a-drink-or-drug-problem.html

Bowlby, J. (1958), 'The nature of the child's tie to his mother', *International Journal of PsychoAnalysis*, XXXIX, 1–23.

Bowlby, J. (1969), *Attachment and Loss, Vol. 1: Attachment.* New York, NY: Basic Books.

Brackett, M. (2019), *Permission to Feel: Unlock the power of emotions to help yourself and your child thrive.* London: Quercus Editions Ltd.

Brey, P. (2012), 'Well-being in philosophy, psychology, and economics', in: P. Brey, A. Briggle and E. Spence (Eds.), *The Good Life in a Technological Age.* Abingdon: Routledge, pp. 15–34.

Brown, B. (2014), 'How to be yourself, even in life's most anxiety-inducing moments', *O, The Oprah Magazine*, www.oprah.com/spirit/brene-brown-advice-how-to-be-yourself/all

Brümmer, V. and Sarot, M. (1996), *Happiness, Well-Being and the Meaning of Life.* Kampen: Kok Pharos Publishing House.

Bruner, J. S. (1960), *The Process of Education.* Cambridge, MA: Harvard University Press.

Calvert, M. and Henderson, J. (1998), *Managing Pastoral Care.* London: Cassell.

Carlquist, E., Nafstad, H. E., Blakar, R. M., Ulleberg, P., Delle Fave, A. and Phelps, J. M. (2017), 'Well-being vocabulary in media language: an analysis of changing word usage in Norwegian newspapers', *The Journal of Positive Psychology*, 12, (2), 99–109.

Carpenter, B. (2020), 'The recovery curriculum: Re-connection, recovery and resilience', www.aaia.org.uk/storage/medialibrary/o_1egifgdnn1n4m1c73ef4rei16uo8.pdf

Caruana, F., Jezzini, A., Sbriscia-Fioretti, B., Rizzolatti, G. and Gallese, V. (2011), 'Emotional and social behaviors elicited by electrical stimulation of the insula in the macaque monkey', *Current Biology*, 21, (3), 195–199.

Center on the Developing Child, 'Resilience', https://developingchild.harvard.edu/science/key-concepts/resilience

Children's Society (2020), 'The good childhood report', www.childrenssociety.org.uk/good-childhood

Clark, A. and Senik, C. (2011), 'Is happiness different from flourishing? Cross-country evidence from the ESS', Working Paper 2011-04. Paris: School of Economics.

Cox, T. (1995), 'Stress, coping and physical health', in: A. Broome and S. Llewelyn (Eds.), *Health Psychology: Process and applications* (2nd edn.). London: Singular Publication Group, pp. 21–35.

Crisp, A. H., Gelder, M. G., Rix, S., Meltzer, H. I. and Rowlands, O. J. (2000), 'Stigmatization of people with mental illnesses', *British Journal of Psychiatry*, 177, 4–7.

Cupit, G. (2007), 'The marriage of science and spirit: Dynamic systems theory and the development of spirituality', *International Journal of Children's Spirituality*, 12, (2), 105–116.

Daft, R. (2008), *The Leadership Experience*. Stamford, CT: Cengage Learning.

Damasio, A. R. (1999), *The Feeling of What Happens: Body and emotion in the making of consciousness*. New York, NY: Harcourt Brace.

Darling-Hammond, L., Zielezinski, M. B. and Goldman, S. (2014), 'Using technology to support at-risk students' learning', www.tes.com/tesv2/files/news-inline/scope-pub-using-technology-report.pdf

Darvin, R. (2016), 'Language and identity in the digital age', in: S. Preece (Ed.), *The Routledge Handbook of Language and Identity*. Abingdon: Routledge, pp. 523–540.

Davey, G. (2018), *Psychology*. Chichester: John Wiley and Sons.

Dellantonio, S. and Pastore, L. (2017), *Internal Perception: The role of bodily information in concepts and word mastery*. Berlin: Springer.

Dellasega, C. and Nixon, C. (2003), *Girl Wars: 12 strategies that will end female bullying*. New York, NY: Simon and Schuster.

Department for Education (2016), 'Funding boost for schools helping pupils develop character', www.gov.uk/government/news/funding-boost-for-schools-helping-pupils-develop-character

Department for Education (2020), 'Personal, social, health and economic (PSHE) education', www.gov.uk/government/publications/personal-social-health-and-economic-education-pshe/personal-social-health-and-economic-pshe-education

Department for Education and Skills (2004), 'Promoting emotional health and well-being through the national healthy school standard'.

Department of Health and Department for Education (2017), 'Transforming children and young people's mental health provision: A green paper', https://assets.publishing.service.gov.uk/government/uploads/system/uploads/attachment_data/file/664855/Transforming_children_and_young_people_s_mental_health_provision.pdf

Desforges, C. and Abouchaar, A. (2003), 'The impact of parental involvement, parental support and family education on pupil achievement and adjustment: a literature review', London: Department for Education and Skills.

Diener, E., Lucas, R., Schimmack, U. and Helliwell, J. (2008), *Well-Being for Public Policy*. Oxford: Oxford University Press.

Dodge, R., Daly, A. P., Huyton, J. and Sanders, L. D. (2012), 'The challenge of defining wellbeing', *International Journal of Wellbeing*, 2, (3), 222–235.

Dolan, P., Peasgood, T. and White, M. (2008), 'Do we really know what makes us happy? A review of the economic literature on the factors associated with subjective well-being', *Journal of Economic Psychology*, 29, (1), 94–122.

Elmer, L. D., MacDonald, D. A. and Friedman, H. L. (2003), 'Transpersonal psychology, physical health, and mental health: Theory, research, and practice', *The Humanistic Psychologist*, 31, (2–3), 159–181.

Emerson, L., Fear, J., Fox, S. and Sanders, E. (2012), 'Parental engagement in learning and schooling: lessons from research', A report by the Australian Research Alliance for Children and Youth (ARACY) for the Family-School and Community Partnerships Bureau: Canberra.

Fehr, B. and Russell, J. A. (1984), 'Concept of emotion viewed from a prototype perspective', *Journal of Experimental Psychology*, 113, 464–486.

Feldman Barrett, L. (2017), *How Emotions Are Made*. London: Macmillan.

Fletcher, G. (2016), *The Routledge Handbook of Philosophy of Well-Being*. Abingdon: Routledge.

Fontana, D. (2011), *Is Christianity Good for You?* Alresford: John Hunt Publishing.

References

Foresight Mental Capital and Wellbeing Project (2008), 'Final project report – executive summary'. London: The Government Office for Science.

Francis, L. J. (1978), 'Attitude and longitude: A study in measurement', *Character Potential: A Record of Research*, 8, (3), 119–130.

Fredrickson, B. L. (2008), 'Promoting positive affect', in: M. Eid and R. J. Larsen (Eds.), *The Science of Subjective Well-being*. New York, NY: Guilford Press, pp. 449–468.

Freshwater, D. (2006), *Mental Health and Illness*. Chichester: John Wiley & Sons.

Gelpi, M. D. (2008), 'Jesuit high schools as communities of character', *Dissertation Abstracts International,* 69, 1721.

Glatzer, W. (2001), 'German sociologists are looking for the "Good Society"', *Social Indicators Research*, 55, 353–359.

Goddard, G., Smith, V. and Boycott, C. (2013), *PSHE in the Primary School*. Abingdon: Routledge.

Goodall, J. and Montgomery, C. (2014), 'Parental involvement to parental engagement: a continuum', *Educational Review*, 66, (4), 399–410.

Government Office for Science (2008), 'Mental capital and wellbeing: making the most of ourselves in the 21st century', www.gov.uk/government/publications/mental-capital-and-wellbeing-making-the-most-of-ourselves-in-the-21st-century

Gowans, C. W. (2015), *Buddhist Moral Philosophy: An introduction*. Abingdon: Routledge.

Green, O. H. (1992), *The Emotions: A philosophical theory*. Dordrecht: Springer Science and Business Media.

Halstead, J. M. and Reiss, M. J. (2003), *Values in Sex Education*. London: RoutledgeFalmer.

Harris, A., Andrew-Power, K. and Goodall, J. (2009), *Do Parents Know They Matter?* London: Continuum.

Harris, A. and Goodall, J. (2007), 'Engaging parents in raising achievement – do parents know they matter?', DCSF Research Report, RW 004.

Hart, A. D. and Hart Frejd, S. (2013), *The Digital Invasion: How technology is shaping you and your relationships*. Grand Rapids, MI: Baker Books.

Hausman, D. M. (2015), *Valuing Health: Well-being, freedom, and suffering*. Oxford: Oxford University Press.

Haybron, D. M. (2008), 'Philosophy and the science of subjective well-being', in: M. Eid and R. J. Larsen (Eds.), *The Science of Subjective Well-being*. New York, NY: Guilford Press, pp. 17–43.

Headmasters' and Headmistresses' Conference (2016), 'Research: teenage use of mobile devices during the night', www.hmc.org.uk/blog/research-teenage-use-mobile-devices-night

Healy, M. (2018), *The Emotionally Healthy Child*. Novato, CA: New World Library.

Heathwood, C. (2017), 'Unconscious pleasures and attitudinal theories of pleasure', *Utilitas*, 30, (2), 219–227.

Helsper, E. J. (2008), *Digital Inclusion: An Analysis of Social Disadvantage and the Information Society*. London: Communities and Local Government.

High, B. (2012), *Bullycide in America*. Darlington, MD: JBS Publishing.

Hockenbury, D. and Hockenbury, S. E. (2007), *Discovering Psychology*. New York, NY: Worth Publishers.

Holden, G. W. (2020), *Parenting: A Dynamic Perspective*. London: Sage.

Holmes, E. (2005), *Teacher Well-being: Looking After Yourself and Your Career in the Classroom*. Abingdon: Routledge.

Hornby, G. and Lafaele, R. (2011), 'Barriers to parental involvement in education: An explanatory model', *Educational Review*, 63, (1), 37–52.

Hoyle, A. and McGeeney, E. (2020), *Great Relationships and Sex Education*. Abingdon: Routledge.

Human Rights Campaign, 'A call to action: LGBTQ youth need inclusive sex education', www.hrc.org/resources/a-call-to-action-lgbtq-youth-need-inclusive-sex-education

James, C., Davis, K., Charmaraman, L., Konrath, S., Slovak, P., Weinstein, E. and Yarosh, L. (2017), 'Digital life and youth well-being, social connectedness, empathy, and narcissism', *Pediatrics*, 140 (Supplement 2), S71–S75.

Jensen, F. E. (2015), *The Teenage Brain: A neuroscientist's survival guide to raising adolescents and young adults*. London: HarperCollins Publishers.

Jernigan, H. L. (2001), 'Spirituality in older adults: A cross-cultural and interfaith perspective', *Pastoral Psychology*, 49, (6), 413–437.

Jordan, B. (2009), 'Blurring boundaries: the "real" and the "virtual" in hybrid spaces', *Human Organization*, 68, (2), 181–193.

Keyes, C. L. M. (1998), 'Social well-being', *Social Psychology Quarterly*, 61, (2), 121–140.

Kleinginna, R. K. and Kleinginna, M. A. (1981), 'A categorized list of emotion definitions, with suggestions for a consensual definition', *Motivation and Emotion*, 5, 345–379.

Leary, M. R. (2004), *The Curse of the Self: Self-awareness, egotism, and the quality of human life*. New York, NY: Oxford University Press.

Lee, W. (1994), *The Spirit with Our Spirit*. Anaheim, CA: Living Stream Ministry.

Leichter, H. J. (1974), 'Some perspectives on family as educator', *Teachers College Record*, 76, (2).

Lickona, T. (1996), 'Eleven principles of effective character education', *Journal of Moral Education*, 25, (1), 93–100.

Livingstone, S. (2017), 'No, the internet is not actually stealing kids' innocence', LSE Blog, https://blogs.lse.ac.uk/parenting4digitalfuture/2017/08/16/no-the-internet-is-not-actually-stealing-kids-innocence

Lomanowska, A. M. and Guitton, M. J. (2012), 'Spatial proximity to others determines how humans inhabit virtual worlds', *Computers in Human Behavior*, 28, (2), 318–323.

Lyubomirsky, S. and Lepper, H. (1999), 'A measure of subjective happiness: preliminary reliability and construct validation', *Social Indicators Research*, 46, 137–155.

Mangal, S. K. and Mangal, U. (2008), *Teaching of Social Studies*. New Delhi: PHI Learning.

Marland, M. (1974), *Pastoral Care*. London: Heinemann.

Maslow, A. H. (1943), 'A theory of human motivation', *Psychological Review*, 50, (4), 370–396.

Maslow, A. H. (1968), *Toward a Psychology of Being*. New York, NY: D. Van Nostrand Company.

McClelland, D. C. (1961), *The Achieving Society*. Princeton, NJ: Van Nostrand.

Mental Health Foundation (2018), 'Mental health statistics: children and young people', www.mentalhealth.org.uk/statistics/mental-health-statistics-children-and-young-people

Mental Health Foundation (2020), 'WWF and the Mental Health Foundation publish mental health support guide', www.mentalhealth.org.uk/campaigns/thriving-with-nature/press-release

Miller, C. 'Does social media cause depression?', Child Mind Institute, https://childmind.org/article/is-social-media-use-causing-depression/

Mora, G. (2008), 'Renaissance conceptions and treatments of madness', in: E. R. Wallace and J. Gach (Eds.), *History of Psychiatry and Medical Psychology*. Boston, MA: Springer, pp. 227–254.

Morgan, N. (2017), *The Teenage Guide to Friends*. London: Walker Books.

Morgan, N. (2018), *The Teenage Guide to Life Online*. London: Walker Books.

Naar, H. and Teroni, F. (2018), *The Ontology of Emotions*. Cambridge: Cambridge University Press.

National Academies of Sciences, Engineering, and Medicine (2017), *Communities in Action: Pathways to health equity*. Washington, DC: The National Academies Press.

Neave, N. (2008), *Hormones and Behaviour: A psychological approach*. Cambridge: Cambridge University Press.

Nelson, J. (2009), *Psychology, Religion and Spirituality*. New York, NY: Springer.

Nielsen, J. (2005), 'Usability of websites for teenagers', http://district4.extension.ifas.ufl.edu/Tech/TechPubs/Usability4Teens.pdf

Nucci, L. P. and Narvaez, D. (2014), *Handbook of Moral and Character Education*. Abingdon: Routledge.

OECD (2013), 'Education at a glance 2013: OECD indicators', www.oecd.org/education/eag2013.htm

Oxford Dictionary of Islam, 'Ruh', www.oxfordislamicstudies.com/article/opr/t125/e2027

Parmar, N. (2017), *Digital Parenting*. Self-published.

Parrish, M. (2014), *Social Work Perspectives on Human Behaviour*, 2nd edn. Maidenhead: Open University Press.

Peterson, P. S. (2017), *The Decline of Established Christianity in the Western World: Interpretations and responses*. Abingdon: Routledge.

Petter, O. (2018), 'Banning children from the internet is like "child abuse", claims sociologist', *Independent*, www.independent.co.uk/life-style/health-and-families/children-internet-ban-child-abuse-parents-sociologist-birmingham-university-a8357221.html

Philpot, T. and Tomlinson, P. (2008), *A Child's Journey to Recovery: Assessment and planning with traumatized children*. London: Jessica Kingsley Publishers.

Piotrowska, P. J., Tully, L. A., Lenroot, R., Kimonis, E., Hawes, D., Moul, C., Frick, P. J., Anderson, V. and Dadds, M. R. (2017), 'Mothers, fathers, and parental systems: a conceptual model of parental engagement in programmes for child mental health–connect, attend, participate, enact (CAPE)', *Clinical Child and Family Psychology Review*, 20, (2), 146–161.

Pollard, E. and Lee, P. (2003), 'Child well-being: a systematic review of the literature', *Social Indicators Research*, 61, (1), 9–78.

Prensky, M. (2001), 'Digital natives, digital immigrants', *On the Horizon*, 9, (5), 1–6.

Railton, P. (1986), 'Facts and values', *Philosophical Topics*, 14, 5–31.

Rath, T. and Harter, J. K. (2010), *Wellbeing: The five essential elements*. New York, NY: Gallup Press.

Rayburn, C. A. (2004), 'Religion, spirituality, and health', *American Psychologist*, 59, (1), 52–53.

Rees, G. and Main, G. (2016), 'Subjective well-being and mental health', in: J. Bradshaw (Ed.), *The Well-Being of Children in the UK*, 4th edn. Bristol: Policy Press, pp. 123–148.

Rogers, C. R. (1961), *On Becoming a Person*. London: Houghton Mifflin.

Safeguarding in Schools, 'What is safeguarding?', www.safeguardinginschools.co.uk/safeguarding-and-governors/what-is-safeguarding

Sailer, R. C. (1931), *Happiness Self-Estimates of Young Men*. New York, NY: Columbia University.

Sarginson, J., Webb, R. T., Stocks, S. J., Esmail, A., Garg, S. and Ashcroft, D. M. (2017), 'Temporal trends in antidepressant prescribing to children in UK primary care, 2000–2015', *Journal of Affective Disorders*, 210, 312–318.

Schrauf, R. W. and Sanchez, J. (2004), 'The preponderance of negative emotion words in the emotion lexicon: A cross-generational and cross-linguistic study', *Journal of Multilingual and Multicultural Development*, 25, (2), 266–284.

Schutte, N. S., Malouff, J. M., Simunek, M., McKenley, J. and Hollander, S. (2002), 'Characteristic emotional intelligence and emotional wellbeing', *Cognition and Emotion*, 16, (6), 769–785.

Scott, D. G. (2009), 'The role of spirituality in human development and identity: An introduction', in: M. de Souza, L. J. Francis, J.

O'Higgins-Norman and D. G. Scott (Eds.), *International Handbook for Spirituality, Care and Wellbeing*. London: Springer, pp. 269–274.

Sieff, D. F. (2015), *Understanding and Healing Emotional Trauma*. Hove: Routledge.

Simmons, R. (2011), *Odd Girl Out*. New York, NY: Mariner Books.

Small, G. and Vorgan, G. (2008), *iBrain: Surviving the technological alteration of the modern mind*. New York, NY: HarperCollins Publishers.

Solomon, R. C. (1976), *The Passions*. Notre Dame, IN: University of Notre Dame Press.

Spahn, A. (2015), 'Can technology make us happy?', in: J. H. Søraker, J.-W. Van der Rijt, J. de Boer, P.-H. Wong and P. Brey (Eds.), *Well-Being in Contemporary Society*. Heidelberg: Springer, pp. 93–113.

Stone, A. and Mackie, C. (2013), *Subjective Well-being: Measuring happiness, suffering, and other dimensions of experience*. Washington, DC: The National Academies Press.

Stubbs, H. (2016), 'Number of children prescribed anti-depressants increases by 50% in seven years', *Independent*, www.independent. co.uk/life-style/health-and-families/health-news/number-children-prescribed-anti-depressants-increases-50-seven-years-a6920576.html

Sumner, L. W. (1996), *Welfare, Happiness and Ethics*. Oxford: Oxford University Press.

Tang, Y. Y. (2017), *The Neuroscience of Mindfulness Meditation: How the body and mind work together to change our behaviour*. Cham: Springer.

Taylor, C. (1991), *The Malaise of Modernity*. Toronto: House of Anansi.

Taylor, T. E. (2012), *Knowing What is Good for You*. London: Palgrave Macmillan.

Taylor, T. E. (2015), 'Towards consensus on well-being', in: J. H. Søraker et al. (Eds.), *Well-Being in Contemporary Society*. Cham: Springer.

Therrien, A. (2018), 'Fifth of 14-year-old girls in UK "have self-harmed"', BBC, www.bbc.co.uk/news/health-45329030

Tiwald, J. (2017), 'Punishment and autonomous shame in Confucian thought', *Criminal Justice Ethics*, 36, (1), 45–60.

UNICEF (2013), 'Child well-being in rich countries: A comparative overview', www.unicef-irc.org/publications/pdf/rc11_eng.pdf

Watson, G. (1930), 'Happiness among adult students of education', *Journal of Educational Psychology*, 21, (2), 79–109.

Watson, D., Clark, L. A. and Tellegen, A. (1988), 'Development and validation of brief measures of positive and negative affect: The PANAS scales', *Journal of Personality and Social Psychology*, 54, (6), 1063–1070.

Waughfield, C. and Burckhalter, T. S. (2002), *Mental Health Concepts*, 5th edn. Stamford, CT: Cengage Learning.

Williams, M. and Penman, D. (2011), *Mindfulness: A practical guide to finding peace in a frantic world*. London: Piaktus.

Wiseman, R. (2002), *Queen Bees and Wannabes*. London: Piatkus Books.

Wood, A. M., Linley, P. A., Maltby, J., Baliousis, M. and Joseph, S. (2008), 'The authentic personality: a theoretical and empirical conceptualization and the development of the authenticity scale', *Journal of Counseling Psychology*, 55, (3), 385–399.

Yang, D. and Zhou, H. (2017), 'The comparison between Chinese and Western well-being', *Open Journal of Social Sciences*, 5, (11), 181–188.

Yarcheski, A., Scoloveno, M. A. and Mahon, N. E. (1994), 'Social support and well-being in adolescents: The role of hopefulness', *Nursing Research*, 43, (5), 288–292.

Your Sexual Health Matters, 'LGBT+', www.yoursexualhealthmatters.org.uk/further-sexual-health-support/lgbt

Index

Index